Florentine Art Treasures

by Rosa Maria Letts

Roydon

This Edition Published by Roydon Publishing Ltd.,
81, Goswell Road, London E.C.1.
English Translation Copyright Roydon Publishing Ltd.
Typesetting by Anytime Artwork,
All Rights Reserved.
Printed in Italy.
I.S.B.N. 0-86288-000-9.

AN INTRODUCTION TO FLORENTINE PAINTING

FLORENCE AND THE DAWN OF THE RENAISSANCE

"The Renaissance happened in Florence when one returned to the forms of the noble and ancient statues and the rules of nature", wrote Lorenzo Ghiberti, a 15th century florentine sculptor, in his 'Commentaries'.

Why it happened in Florence is difficult to establish, but is was there that at the beginning of the 15th century a group of artists started looking at the world and the people around them as they were to represent them in their works.

They were partially stimulated by the interest shown towards the classical culture by some writers and poets, like Francesco Petrarch, during the previous century. These scholars had read the works of Greek and Roman writers and philosophers and had looked at the remains of classical sculptures and buildings. They had sensed in them and their artists a vigorous appreciation of nature, man and physical life, until now considered contrary to the beliefs of the Christian tradition. These writers who were true and sincere Christians themselves then rediscovered in the Christian doctrine those elements of celebration of man and human nature that it contained.

Correspondingly, when the few artists influenced by this new more natural outlook started looking around them to take inspiration from nature, they could not help noticing the beauty of creation. Imagine the green hills of Tuscany bathed by the magic light and warm glow of the Mediterranean sun. These can be recognised in the backgrounds of Donatello's sculptures.

Try and imagine the beautiful women of the Florentine countryside, the amber tonality of their complexions, the direct intense stare of their brown eyes, their firm taut limbs accustomed to work in the fields and carrying proudly their babies whilst they worked. These you will recognise amongst the crowds and holy characters of Masaccio's frescoes.

Think of the streets and squares of Florence, recently benefiting from a period of the slum clearance when space was created around their newly built cathedral and the massive but elegant government buildings, the Palazzo Vecchio. They will appear behind the paintings of Brunelleschi or Masolino.

This phenomenon of re-appreciation of the human aspects of life considered now as God's gift to mankind and not as a punishment or a period of transition before reaching a better life, came to reshape man's values. The whole phenomenon was rightly called 'the Rebirth' or 'the Renaissance'.

It is appropriate to start our survey of Florentine Painting with the works of Giotto di Bondone (1266-1336).

He could be called the first Italian universal artist, forerunner of that renaissance ideal of a many-sided genius. Painter, sculptor and architect, Giotto was the first European artist since classical times to paint with vivid realism and a bold sense of volume so different to the Gothic art still practiced all over Europe.

In 1296, as assistant to Cimabue, he worked on the frescoes in the naves of the Upper Church of San Francis in Assisi. Giotto must have felt unable to interpret the humble simple life of the poor man of Assisi with the gold grounds and spiked pinnacles of the gothic iconography.

'Be praised, O Lord, for Brother Wind
and for air and cloud, for fair and for
all weather by which Thou givest Thy
creatures sustenance.
Be praised, O Lord, for Sister Water,
the which is so useful, humble, precious
and chaste',

San Francis had said, and Giotto tried to translate his very words into visual image. Within a clear and vibrant outline he enclosed images of unsurpassed reality. Their strong contours isolate them from their backgrounds, still rendered rather crudely. Their strong sense of volume makes them stand out vigorously while the warm tonality of their colours, which range from the ivories to the pinks, terracottas and browns, adds warmth and humanity to the scenes.

It is the world of the Franciscan community which is described here in its entirety. The Poor Brothers with their weathered faces, baked by the sun or dried by the winds and cold weather which they had to face during their charitable peregrinations, appear in Giotto's narration just as they must have been in real life. Framed by their dark hoods, silhouetted in their simple tunics against rocky unfriendly landscapes, one can share in the harshness of the Friars' lives.

In 1304 Giotto was invited to Padua to fresco the Arena chapel. Built by Enrico degli Scrovegni as an offering to God against his father's sins of usury, this is perhaps the pictorial masterpiece of the artist.

In it the stories of the Life of the Virgin, Saint Anne and Saint Joachim are told with a new vitality and great unity of form and content. Each image is once again outlined by a strong black contour which seems to isolate it from the rest of the composition. Nonetheless, this very line manages to create space, to suggest perspective and volume. The landscape is still painted naively, as in a story tale. The relation between people and objects is still hierarchical, following the medieval fashion. Hence beside a majestic Joachim we find a tree or a bush hardly larger than his own arm. Yet not even this seems to detract from the veracity of the scene represented. Giotto's bold human figures bring to the art of painting a new sincerity, a new persuasiveness.

*'Credette Cimabue nella pittura
tener lo campo, ed ora ha Giotto
il grido, si che la fama di colui
é oscura'.*

(Cimabue believed to hold the field in painting and now Giotto has renown, so that the glory of the former is dimmed), Dante says in the eleventh Canto of the Purgatory in his Divine Comedy, confirming Giotto's success among his contemporaries.

Giotto was by the second decade of the fourteenth century the first painter in Italy to acquire fame on a national scale. He was invited to paint in Rome, Naples and Milan. The ruling body of Florence, the Signoria, made him 'Overseer of Works for the Cathedral', the most important honour which the town could bestow on an artist. During the last years of his life (1317 onwards) he painted the frescoes of another cycle on the Life of Saint Francis in the Bardi chapel in the Church of Santa Croce, Florence. (Ill. 1 & 2). The old theme, taken up again in his later years, confronts us with a more volumetric handling of the scheme leaving us some unforgettable compositions, like the one of the 'Dream of Saint Francis' (Ill.2).

After Giotto's death, until at least the end of the century, the art of painting in Florence appears to have fallen into a persistent decline. Many painters, some 'followers of Giotto' as they wanted to be called. — 'the Giotteschi' — tried to imitate the master and his manner without a real understanding of his art. They copied his style, the bold contours, his colours, even his defects, but none of their works have that sparkle of vitality and truth which turns Giotto's paintings into 'art'. Among the more accomplished followers are Bernado Daddi and Andrea da Firenze. The poverty of followers, however, was also due to the Black Death which stormed across Tuscany in the mid-fourteenth century, decimating the artists as well as the rest of the population.

Nearly a century passed before Giotto's art was continued by an artist of comparable ability, Masaccio. However, before approaching his work,we will have to outline the magnificent artistic phenomenon which took place in Florence, around the beginning of the fifteenth century, and which affected all aspects of its cultural life. It came to be called 'The Renaissance'.

BRUNELLESCHI, DONATELLO AND MASACCIO AND THE BEGINNING OF 'RENAISSANCE ART'

To start our survey of Florentine Renaissance Paintings, we must examine two lost panels painted by Filippo Brunelleschi around 1415-1420. Filippo, the future architect of the dome of Florence Cathedral, started his career as a sculptor. Having lost to Lorenzo Ghiberti the competition to build a new set of bronze doors for the Baptistry of Florence, he left or Rome, where he dedicated himself to the study of classical art and architecture. There he tried to learn the building techniques of the Romans.

To discover the secrets which made possible the erection of such massive structures as the Pantheon or the Colyseum became the greatest challenge to his inquisitive mind. He drew plan after plan, constructed model after model in order to find out how the Romans could have erected the Pantheon. This is nothing more than a huge dome resting on the ground. These plans eventually enabled him to build a dome of similar size, but suspended 180 feet above the ground, on the drum of Florence Cathedral.

The sketches and designs that Brunelleschi needed to illustrate his architectural projects must have needed careful rendering of dimensions and distances. The artist must have appreciated then how difficult it was to give a real sense of space or distance on flat surfaces without a consistent system of perspective. In the two panels which he painted around 1415, immediately after his return to Florence, he applied for the first time a new method of perspective called centralised or, one-point perspective. Its main feature was the arrangement of all parts and elements of the composition along ideal directional lines all converging on a focal point.

The two panels represented views of the squares, roads and buildings which could be seen from a door of Florence Cathedral and from the main door of Palazzo Vecchio, the seat of the Florentine government. Using the doors as frames to enclose his subject matter, the artist jotted down whatever was in front of his eyes. It seems that Brunelleschi covered the ground of the panel with burnished silver to obtain a mirror effect. In the panel he then outlined the buildings reflected there. He also translated all the visual distortions created by distance and angle, such as making things smaller the further they were from him. With this procedure Brunelleschi obtained a mirror image of the scene in front of him. Perhaps this is why he inserted a hole at the focal point of the composition and asked the viewer to look through it from the back holding a mirror on the far side so that the painting was reflected in it. The beholder would then be able to see all the elements of the composition, diminished or foreshortened as they appeared to the artist when he stood in the doorway of the Cathedral.

The two works must have been of great artistic interest but also of tremendous importance for the development of painting, something which Filippo's contemporaries did not fail to recognise. Thus Leon Battista Alberti, the painter, architect and theoretician of the early renaissance in 1435 dedicated his Treaty 'On Painting' to Brunelleschi

> "... for what I understood in (the works of)
> many, but above all in you, Filippo and in
> that great friend of yours Donato (Donatello),
> the sculptor, and in that other Nencio (Ghiberti)
> and Luca (della Robbia) and Masaccio ..."

At the end of this dedication Alberti refers to Masaccio, that is Tommaso of Ser Giovanni (1401-1428), who was the first really great painter of the Renaissance. Together with Donatello he was Brunelleschi's greatest friend. If it had not been for the close association among these artists, Florentine Renaissance art at this point would not have concerned itself with so many and varied problems. Since they were not only concerned with a more realistic rendering of events, something which Giotto had started before them, but with the rendering of space, perspective, plasticity, ie:- three dimensionality, and a new inner logic of composition.

What this young artistic milieu was really attempting was to entrust art with the new engaging role of interpreting reality. They, therefore, first of all had to unravel it.

The study and examination of nature and life became for the visual artist, as it had already been for the poets and humanists, the centre of their inquiry. To this attentive quest, nature and life appeared in all their complexity, with all their virtues and defects, fullness and emptiness, happiness and wretchedness.

What we find then in Florence, around the second decade of the 15th century, is the first group of 'intellectual artists'. They were no longer craftsmen just interested in the execution of traditional images, but men facing certain problems, formulating certain concepts and trying to share them through their works with the public. That is why, almost for the first time since the end of classical art, we find again artists engaged in writing theoretical treatises, like Leonbattista Alberti, who wrote works 'On Painting', 'On Sculpture' and 'On Architecture'. Also we find artists and historians engaged with the writing of artists' biographies, now considered interesting enough to become the subject of literary compositions.

It was this very reason that brought Giorgio Vasari, himself a painter and architect, to write during the following century 'The Lives of the Most Excellent Italian Painters, Sculptors and Architects'. The book, normally known as 'The Lives of the Artists', remains to this day the basis of any study of Italian Renaissance art. In spite of its bias and incongruity, it is a most vivid account of the development of Renaissance art.

In Florence, in the small osterie (wine cellars), we can visualise our artists gathering during the hot summer evenings, to discuss their beliefs and theories, to formulate their artistic techniques. In so doing they started that form of artistic discussions which still passionately involves so many scholars, critics, historians and connoisseurs. From a purely manual activity, art became an intellectual pre-occupation. The pre-occupation of these men to understand and represent 'nature' and 'man' led them to scientific and technical experiments. In order to learn how to represent man and his environment, the study of mathematics, geometry, optics and anatomy were pursued. Thus the foundations of the modern era were laid.

Greeks and Romans were well in advance of the medieval artists in their knowledge of anatomy and space rendering. After all, their artistic interest had been centred round the human body, movement and the representation of the world of nature. They even tried to represent the elements. Think for instance of those hellenistic sculptures of 'the winds' — those magnificent ethereal goddesses who seem to glide through space, embraced by draperies softly swaying around their slender limbs. Such was the mastery of the Greek sculptors over the treatment of marble, that their chisels do not seem to cut into the stone but to mould it. The technical knowledge they had of their media and the tools they developed for its working were highly sophisticated. It was natural for the artists of the first Renaissance to turn to their classical predecessors to admire and learn from them.

Their own approach to nature and man, however, moved from another angle. And here the Christian component, ie:- the influence of the Christian teaching of the 'dark ages' lent a new perspective. What the Renaissance artist was concerned with was not the human body and its exploits, but man and the human spirit. Herein lies the main difference between classical and Renaissance art. The first represents man through the expression of his physical characteristics, the second aims at representing him through his spiritual qualities.

Classical art, therefore, represents the physical aspects of man in the most favourable light. Accordingly the body will be shown in beauty — young, athletic and in movement. While the Renaissance, in representing the human being, sees beauty in old age as well as in youth; describes sorrow as well as happiness. Its art, in an attempt to express the depth of human feelings, values stillness as well as movement and the sympathetic wrinkles of an old face as much as the fresh charm of a young one.

We thus find Donatello sculpting in his youth the vigorous young body of the David, the Saint George and the young putti of the Cantoria of Florence Cathedral. While in his maturity he created the most unforgettable expression of an aged humanity, as in the Magdalene of the Baptistery in Pisa or the grieved Maries of the Deposition panel from the pulpit of the Church of San Lorenzo.

Brunelleschi who started his career with the slender agile profile of the Dome of Florence Cathedral and the linear elegant plan of the Church of S. Lorenzo produced, before dying, the complex, volumetric plan of the Church of S. Spirito.

Masaccio finally, even within the three examples of his work which appear in this volume, moves from the over expressive grimaces of the characters in the Naples' crucifixion to the restrained grief of the aged Mary in the fresco of S. Maria Novella. (Ill. 3 & 5).

Thus Florence spoke at the beginning of the 15th century through the voice of its first Renaissance artists. Theirs remain to this day the more understandable of all artistic messages. It so happened that death prematurely arrested the fluid brush of Masaccio for he died in 1428 aged 27. As had already happened after Giotto's death, even though many great painters were contributing to the art of the period, only a few were able to understand the great innovations inherent in the stark simplicity of his images, in the wide severe spaces of his backgrounds. His social awareness of the beauty of mankind, even in its simplest and most humble form, makes him the first painter of a new modern manner.

THE PAINTERS OF THE EARLY RENAISSANCE

Abandoning momentarily Masaccio's stark realism, the Florentine masters of the early 15th century followed many other paths in the pursuit of a style of painting more realistic than the medieval or gothic. The typical spirit of the Florentines, individualistic and experimental, meant that they left few stones unturned.

From 1430 onwards, a large number of painters enlisted among the guild of Physicians and Pharmacists to which they belonged. Among these were Masolino, Beato Angelico, Filippo Lippi, Paolo Uccello and many others. It is hard to believe that so many great talents could find themselves at the same time, in the same place, to serve the same Muse. Each developed a different manner, attracted by an original technique, and chose opposite subject matters within the framework of a renewed, reborn, artistic inspiration.

Hence we would find side by side with Masaccio, the still linear elegance of Masolino (Florence 1384 - unknown). These two painters worked together on the frescoes of the stories of the Life of Christ and the Apostles in the Brancacci Chapel in the Church of the Carmelite Fathers. Masolino's work has been underestimated by the critics because of being continuously compared with that of Masaccio. Masolino's art derives from subtle chromatic contrasts obtained with the use of luminous, bright hues, refined melodious figures silhouetted against fairy tale skies of cobalt blue. Masolino is like a bridge which tries to bring together the two banks of fourteenth and fifteenth century art. On the one side can be found still present in his paintings the echo of the Senese school of Duccio and Simone Martini in his gold and gem-like colours, in his melodious gothic line full of soft and pervasive musicality. On the other side one can sense his consciousness of space and perspective, his attempts to define the environments of his scenes, even though at times without success. Some of his figures manage to give us a real sense of form and volume through the correct use of light and shade. Take, for instance, the Salome of Castiglion d'Olona (fig.7) where the intense highlighted tonality of the skin models her features with subtle perception.

Contemporary with Masolino are two painters, slightly younger, who both learnt their art since childhood in the quiet of their monasteries. Fra' (Brother) Giovanni da Fiesole, called Beato Angelico and Fra' (Brother) Filippo Lippi. Beato Angelico (1387-1455) entered the Dominican order at a very young age to dedicate himself 'to the greater glory of God' ('ad majorem gloriam dei'), as he himself used to say. As a young man he had spent many hours illustrating sacred and learned books for the library of his monastery. He started painting as a book illuminator but eventually he dedicated the greater part of his artistic life to frescoing the walls of the Monastery of San Marco which Cosimo de' Medici had had rebuilt for the Dominican Brothers on one side of the Via Larga (Broad Way). On the opposite side of the same road was Cosimo's town house, the Medici palace.

Fra' Giovanni, while decorating the walls of the Monastery, was elected to become its Prior. A hard task indeed, for the artist who quietly, within its cells, was creating 'ad majorem gloria dei', perhaps the greatest series of frescoes on the Life and Miracles of Christ (fig. 9.10.11.12.)

To wander among the corridors and cells of the Monastery of San Marco is like losing oneself along a path steeped in divine light. The colours used by the artist to describe the dramatic events of Jesus's life are such that could only have been conceived by his spirit. The scenes are described simply, although vividly, with the faith and truth of a believer who seems to understand everything about the story of heaven for which he is preparing himself. Angelico is accused by the early biographers (Vasari) to be still using gold grounds and bejewelled pastel shades. Yet his spaces and backgrounds ring strangely true. One never questions his countryside and mountains or his too luminous skies, since they share the heightened intensity of his religious narrative. More than the physical world, he tries to render the metaphysical, that world whose existence is beyond and above our own. Somehow the paintings of Angelico seem to bring it so close.

When the story is cruel, more human than divine, Angelico finds accents of extreme intensity and drama. Looking at the San Marco's 'Mocking of Christ' (fig.13) the figure of 'The King of the Jews' appears most vulnerable, protected only by the soft folds of his white tunic. The nobility of the blindfolded face, the luminous hair just balancing on the line of his shoulder, seems to show how unprotected he really is. Meanwhile hands from a ghostly crowd hit him with the added cruelty of anonymous blows. These seem to re-echo against the blue background, while the head of only one man whose eyes are unexpectedly pitiful, is shown spitting and insulting him without much conviction. The painter consciously reacts by strengthening Christ's clasp around his mock sceptre.

In the Prayer in the Garden (fig.14) Fra' Angelico reminds us of Giotto in the naive rendering of the landscape where each character is conceived in isolation within his own contours. Perhaps in this way the artist tries to manifest that feeling of utter solitude which Christ felt during that endless night when he kept awakening his disciples begging in vain that they should not fall asleep.

In all of Fra' Angelico's compositions, even the most sumptuous where God and the Virgin often appear in majesty, on golden thrones, amidst a mass of Angels, Archangels, Patriarchs — richly attired, solemn, divinely beautiful — we can always sense the fundamental sobriety of his message.

Just a few years younger than Beato Angelico is Fra' Filippo Lippi (1406-1469), the well-known Carmelite brother, the painter of so many delightful Madonnas. Filippo who entered the Carmelite order too young because he was orphaned and alone in the world, lived in that very convent where around 1425 Masaccio and Masolino had been frescoing the Stories of the Life and Miracles of Jesus.

Attracted to the practice of painting since childhood, he grew up with a full appreciation of life, almost too curious of what was going on in the world outside the convent. His little escapades into this world were a little too frequent not to displease his superiors. Cosimo de' Medici however, always the friend, often the patron of the Florentine artists, protected the young man in many ways. Hoping that the Brother's interests outside the convent were largely of an artistic nature, Cosimo gave him a workshop in town. Situated in the Via Larga, not far from the Medici residence, halfway between the convent and the palace, the location was rather unfortunate for the too human Brother.

The paintings of Filippo Lippi in fact, perhaps true to the artist's character, are like an outpouring of joy. In them one finds the most beautiful Madonnas with the finest features and the most melodious smiles; the plumpest and rosiest puttis, their budding lips eager not so much to smile as to laugh with an irrepressible joie-de-vivre. In the frescoes which he executed for the Cathedral in Prato we find the most complete expression of Lippi's style.

It was while frescoing in Prato that the artist was asked to paint an altarpiece for a local Monastery. There he fell in love with a young nun whom he saw in the shaded portico of the cloister. Troubles were to be expected. Eventually the Medici's providential intervention obtained the Pope's dispensation so that both young people were allowed to abandon the religious life and could be married. A very happy, laughing 'putto', the future Filippino Lippi, was the result of their union.

BOTTICELLI, GHIRLANDAIO AND PIERO DI COSIMO: THE ARTISTS OF LORENZO'S COURT

Let us dwell for a moment on the paintings of Sandro Botticelli (1444-1510), the greatest exponent of the art of Lorenzo's lifetime. Botticelli, like Giotto, uses design in the modelling of his figures. This is rendered with a wiry, nervous, effervescent line which can be traced and followed all over his panels, but the artist applies it with a technique which makes it almost transparent. His contours are 'engraved' on the paintings with the silverpoint. Thus they effectively disappear when they are coloured over. The colours he uses are like rich enamels, iridescent and brilliant, surcharged with light. The veils draped around his Madonnas are as light and transparent as air, they have the consistency — or inconsistency — of a breeze.

A pupil of Filippo Lippi, Botticelli did part of his apprenticeship in the workshop of Verrocchio, the bronze sculptor and painter who was a favourite artist of Lorenzo de Medici. In the same workshop were also working as assistants Leonardo da Vinci and Lorenzo di Credi. Botticelli, greatly attracted to the elegant and worldly world of Lorenzo, was also influenced by the poetry of Pulci and Politian, the two favourite poets of the Magnifico. Angelo Politian was a famous Greek and Latin scholar and a member of Lorenzo's Neoplatonic academy.

He may have inspired many of the themes of Botticelli's mythological compositions such as 'The Spring', 'The Birth of Venus' or 'Minerva and the Centaur'. In these more complex panels we recognize one of the greatest qualities of Botticelli's art, his sense of composition. As Berenson put it, "Botticelli's art develops in a continuous alteration of perfect form with perfect rhythm". Each element in his scenes seem to be held in an almost magical balance, as they are all co-ordinated towards the centre in perfectly structured arrangements. The 'Mars and Venus' of the National Gallery, London, is a prime example of such balanced harmony.

Another work which is one of the greatest compositions of this period is Alessio Baldovinetti's (1422-1499) Virgin of the Louvre (ill.38). This is perhaps one of the purest, most beautiful images of the Virgin ever painted. Silhouetted against a landscape where the Arno valley appears framed by the Tuscan hills, the Virgin, suave and stately in the foreground, her hands in prayer look adoringly at her baby. The perfect oval of her face, the shape of her neckline, the curve of her shoulders, all harmonize sympathetically and are re-echoed in the undulating background. The transparent veil which frames her face, the sensitive light which radiates from her smile all tell us to which school this artist belongs.

Another witness and narrator of Florentine lifestyle in the latter part of the 15th century is Domenico Ghirlandaio (1445-1494). His chronicle deals with the private, daily lives of the Florentine bourgeoisie. At times a little fragmented and with too much incidental matter, Ghirlandaio's art, in the picture illustrated here (fig. 39) the 'Grandfather and Grandchild' of the Louvre, seems to capture the language of pure art. The perfectly symmetric frame of the window seems to contain and reinforce the embrace which links child and man in a rapport of reciprocal unequivocal tenderness. Each element of the composition, the human, architectural and the natural, combine with each other in a flow of sentiment which turns them into parts of the same organism.

Many other names have enriched the group of the great painters of this period. Filippino Lippi (1457-1504) the most faithful pupil of Botticelli and son of Filippo Lippi, does not seem to be able to capture the great compositive qualities of his master. His best works were achieved in Rome where in the Church of Santa Maria Sopra Minerva are to be found his most spontaneous and effervescent expressions.

Before abandoning this survey of the artists of the last decades of the 15th century, let us look at one last image, symbol of the abrupt end which suddenly struck the whole of the Laurentian society. This is the sublime, classical form of the Simonetta Vespucci by Piero di Cosimo (1462-1521). In this painting, the last to represent the beautiful Simonetta, married very young into a leading Florentine family and killed by an unrecognised illness at 21, silence seems to have fallen heavy on her bare shoulders. This work is not typical of the style of Piero di Cosimo. More often his compositions are filled with a number of mythological themes, treated in a grotesque way such as strange creatures half-man half-beast or scenes of fires or exodus from threatening woods or shores. It is as if in these works, Piero has a presentment of things to come.

Savonarola's Thunderous cry of repentance to the Florentines, the sudden death of Lorenzo the Medici at the age of 45, the subsequent expulsion of the Medici from Florence three years later, will soon prove how right his presentments were.

However, in this work there is no sign of the equivocal treatments which will follow. Simonetta, beloved, if only platonically, by Guilano de Medici, was a symbol of grace, elegance, and beauty. Here the perfect equilibrium between natural and human element, the perfect symmetry of the composition, the sober tonality of colour, the firm underlying drawing give tremendous stability and unity to the works. Every form is re-echoed by another, as the shawl repeating the soft curve of the shoulders, which in turn is continued in the line of hills that can be seen just above the village. Simonetta's perfect profile is re-echoed by the black cloud symbol of her early death. The sad message incorporated in the painting — a posthumous portrait — is reinforced in the clasp of the adder surrounding the young woman's neck. In all this dark symbolism, only the noble forehead and pure features of Simonetta offer themselves — luminous and serene — as an early dawn against the dark background. What better work to introduce us to the climax of Florentine painting: the classical forms of the art of Leonardo, Michelangelo and Raphael.

The change from the solemn hieratic art of the early 15th century to the works of the middle century is as dramatic as the change from black and white to technicolour in the modern cinema. One is almost overwhelmed by the bright chromatic effects and it is hard to single out, at first sight, the main elements of a composition, from the richness and intricacies of the narrative details.

This change occurred in Florence around 1460 when the artists seem to shun the rigorous and sober themes of the previous decades. Hauser, the historian who has concerned himself in depth with the social history of art, attributes this difference of approach to the change which took place in Florentine society at this time. The town was no more run by that first generation of merchants, bankers and businessmen who had helped to develop its economy, but by the next generation. In other words, it is the generation of Lorenzo 'the Magnificent' rather than his plainer, sober grandfather Cosimo; of the ostentious Luca Pitti rather than his scholarly grandfather. It was not the generation who had made the great fortunes who were the basis of Florence's flourishing economy, but their descendants who were better at using those fortunes than at making them.

To describe and interpret their splendid style of life, full of jousts and tournaments, carnivals and all types of public ceremonies; to render their courtly manners, extravagant costumes, exacting protocol and conventions, there was a new generation of painters with an eye for rich patterns, extravagant compositions and exuberant colours!

Benozzo Gozzoli (1420-1479) has left us one of the most attractive examples of this style — strangely close to the previous international gothic — in his fresco of the Adoration of the Kings in the chapel of the Medici Palace. (Ill 32.) Along the walls of the family chapel, in this 15th century palace, are four generations of Medici followed by their courtiers and friends, the poets and humanists of their entourages.

The fresco had to be a reproduction of the way some of them had appeared for the historical meeting held in Florence in 1439 between the Greek Orthodox and the Church of Rome. This had been one of the first attempts to bring the two churches together.

In the frescoes we thus see the Patriarch of Constantinople riding with the Pope and the penultimate Emperor of Constantinople — the Holy Roman Emperor John Paleologus — whose brother was to lose Constantinople to the Turks within five years. In the painted procession we see some of the Greek scholars who had come in their retinues. In this occasion they formed lasting relationships with the Italian humanists and after the fall of Constantinople were soon to make the return journey to Italy.

The event, in which the Medici for the first time had acted — as hosts — in a public role for Italy, proved of extreme importance, not so much for the history of the Church but for the history of European culture.

For the first time since the middle ages, the dialogue between East and West was open again. Within the walls of Constantinople the last teachings and texts of the classical world of Greece and Rome had been treasured during all these centuries. Without the rediscovery of this great past culture, the great art of the High Renaissance, the paintings and buildings of Raphael and Michelangelo, the new architecture of Saint Peter with Michelangelo's dome would have been inconceivable.

But to return to the event from which everything started, let us look at Gozzoli's eastern parade. The artist paints his exotic cavalcade with an aura of enchantment to be found previously in gothic chivalric tales or in the Oriental fables. Near the Eastern Grandees and the Princes of the Church of Rome, the Medici are represented through four successive generations in a cavalcade oblivious of time and place, but not of their relentless social ascent. We thus find Giovanni, Cosimo and Piero plainly dressed and mounted amidst a crowd of friends and followers while their descendants, Giuliano and Lorenzo, are singled out among the princes of Christianity. More richly attired than any of them, on magnificent berberry horses covered in gilt brocade and gem studded fineries, these young men were no mere merchant's sons but Princes.

In our illustration (fig. 32) Giuliano, Lorenzo the Magnificent's younger brother, looks straight at us. He wears a short blue tunic and holds a cheetah from the Medici's own zoo. What a fine example he presents of that glittering world of the Florentine Renaissance at that moment in time.

Perhaps the display of etiquette so well rendered by Gozzoli may have slowly become of paramount importance for the young Medicis, the leaders of taste, culture and artistic patronage in the Florence of the late 15th century. Cosimo's relentless but unshowy form of patronage was continued in a more refined but still restrained manner by his son Piero, a great lover of miniatures and gems, coins, medals and other small artistic items. His love of small artistic objects may have been due to his being confined to a chair by gout. Piero's son Lorenzo, instead, had a reputation for great artistic patronage which was not fully justified by the amount of works he commissioned.

Nonetheless he unquestionably influenced the artistic taste of his lifetime by his own personal style and preferénces. Thus we find that form in art becomes more and more important. The love of decoration and detail in so many compositions corresponds to the Medici's sense of display in public life. Colour chooses the tonalities of gems moving away from the ivories and ambers, terracottas and soft blues of Giotto and Masaccio or the richer yet still soft palettes of Masolino, Angelico and Lippi, for the shiny iridescent hues of Gozzoli, Botticelli and Ghirlandaio.

THE HIGH RENAISSANCE OR THE CLASSICAL AGE OF FLORENTINE PAINTING

The Italian High Renaissance is a uniquely fortunate period in the history of art in that it was a time of great artistic inspiration which had at its disposal the most developed artistic techniques and the most perfect and varied artistic formulas developed during the previous century.

This period is brief, lasting no more than 40 years from about 1480 until 1520, and represented the years of greatest maturity and highest artistic invention of the three great representatives of that style, Leonardo da Vinci, Michelangelo Buonarroti and Raffaello Sanzio. Many other artists and often great ones are working at the same time throughout Italy, but it is in the art of these three geniuses that we find the attainment of perfection.

LEONARDO DA VINCI

For Leonardo da Vinci (1452-1519) painting, as he wrote himself, was the lesser of his talents. For him to paint must have been as easy as to write, in fact easier, since he used to write from left to right! To draw was his normal method of expression, as can be seen looking through his notebooks. He was a draughtsman, a painter, but above all — as he would have it — a scientist.

His own writings may give us a clue as to why his pictures seem more than just beautiful works of art. Rather, they appear to be experiments at representing some natural phenomena. In his own notebooks Leonardo explains how he used to observe nature whose subtle variations he tried to capture in his drawings.

"Just as the flame colours the air which surrounds it, so it illuminates the people and objects around. Its light plays strongly on those parts which face it and gradually sinks into shadow the parts which are further away from the source of light. And this" Leonardo continues "does not happen abruptly, since darkness can only take over when light has let go."

He notes consequently an intermediate area of every varying intensity, brighter when light predominates over darkness and more obscure when darkness takes over. This he calls 'penumbra' — half-shade. In order to be able to render this natural phenomenon in his paintings, he evolved one of the most important artistic techniques which he himself brought to its maximum development: the chiaroscuro or the mixed use of light and shade.

In rendering human forms, he was greatly helped by a highly developed sense of beauty, a beauty heightened by intelligence and sensitivity. It is this spiritual dimension which differentiates his subjects from the ones of any other painter. Looking at his Madonnas or angels or his portraits through their magnificent features, we see their spirit being disclosed. In order to achieve this, Leonardo developed another technique, the sfumato — a shading of surfaces which creates a hollowing effect, adding to their countenance the depth of a searching soul, the mystery of a spiritual yearning. An example of this technique can be found in the features of the St. Anne — in the Cartoon of the Virgin and St. Anne of the National Gallery — or among the faces of old men from the Adoration of the Kings in the Uffizi Gallery (Ill.43).

Further more Leonardo sets his figures in landscapes which, because of his intimate knowledge of nature, he paints with truth and conviction. The dialogue between light and darkness is fundamental to the compositions. Light is used to reveal places in their full existence and darkness to express nature's mysteries. The same light-effects are used to enlighten his human faces, either resplendent in the dewy looks of youth or hazy in the grey shadows of old age. The 'sfumato' allows him to endow those faces with the mystery behind which human intelligence is often screened, while leaving to nature the mystery of its origin and of the intelligence behind its creation.

MICHELANGELO BUONARROTI

Twenty years younger than Leonardo, Michelangelo (1475-1564) is the next great all round artist of the High Renaissance, Sculptor, painter and architect in this order — according to him. We, however, find it impossible to agree since it is impossible to grade perfection. How can one choose between his marble pietas, the frescoes in the Sistine Ceiling or the Dome of St. Peter?

Our interest is confined to his 'painting' which art, for reasons different to Leonardo's, he also considered the least of his talents. 'Michelangelo Buonarroti, sculptor' thus Michelangelo used to sign his works. In order to make him paint the Sistine Ceiling, Pope Julius II had to use every possible threat and trick. The Pope being the stronger, Michelangelo decided to give in and start painting what is perhaps the greatest religious cycle of frescoes of all times.

Michelangelo's art is another example of a form which perfectly expresses its subject. No matter how ambitious or dramatic is the artist's theme and Michelangelo's themes were very ambitious indeed, no matter how desperate the message, Michelangelo would always find the most suitable form for its expression. The breadth of his concepts was such that he could rarely fit them within the narrow frame of one picture.

Michelangelo is known to have painted only one picture, the Holy Family, also called the Tondo Doni. (Ill.45). Two others are attributed to him, the Entombment and the Madonna and Child with St. John and Angels, both in the National Gallery. His ambitious themes were better suited to the vast expanse of large walls or ceilings or to the hardness of the marble blocks.

Michelangelo's paintings are to his frescoes what Beethoven's sonatas are to his symphonies. Even within their reduced dimensions, the breadth of their message is unimpaired.

Looking at the Holy Family the work seems almost made up of two different parts. In the classical background we see a semi-circular wall against which are a group of naked youths.

Arranged as they are, along a horizontal plane, they remind us of the marble frieze of a Greek temple or a Roman sarcophagus. Their indifference to what happens around them a low white wall severs them from the scene in the foreground. Here Mary, sitting on her knees, leans against Joseph as she turns to take the baby. In the sudden twisting movement the Virgin appears strong and beautiful, the ideal Mother of God. The baby is the logical link between the two main characters, the reason for their coming together. Biblically and artistically, in Michelangelo's work, here is the clue to the whole story. The small boy behind the wall — the little St. John — still belongs to the classical world represented there but with the perception of innocence looks adoringly towards baby Jesus thus linking the past pagan era to the future era of Christianity.

Michelangelo is almost the first artist, since Fra' Beato Angelico, to be consistently concerned with the world of Divinity. However, while Angelico looks at it in devotional terms without questions and with the absolute acceptance of what is to come, Michelangelo looks at it in human forms. He almost makes himself the spokesman of humanity in his need to question. He desperately wants to understand "Where do we come from, where are we going? How close or how far are we from God? How similar". He is aware of man's unique gift, unlike other creatures, to create like God. He knows the effort and the strain of the creative process, but also the joy and fulfilment. Who better equipped than him to find out what humanity is all about? And yet he can find no answer.

In the frescoes for the Sistine Ceiling, in a series of magnificent scenes, he describes the whole process of God's creation. For God himself he finds the most perfect image in the strong powerful bearded figure. He appears swiftly moving through the successive stages of creation, surrounded and supported by angels. He is all energy and all wisdom as we follow him in biblical succession as in the creation of the earth, the sun, the moon, the waters and finally the first man and woman.

The cycle accomplished, Michelangelo is finally allowed to return to his beloved marble. The Pope himself entrusts him with the sculptures for his own tomb. A project involving more than 60 life size statues was started, never to be finished. The Pope's death and the unco-operative involvement of his own family with the project was partly to blame for this. However Michelangelo continued to sculpture for the next Pope, Leo X, second son of Lorenzo de Medici.

For this Pope and his family, he was entrusted with a series of statues for the tombs of Lorenzo and Giuliano de' Medici in the Sacristy of San Lorenzo. For these tombs he carved the magnificent figures of Dawn and Dusk, Night and Day to represent the irrevocable passing of time. The artist tried with these statues to satisfy his need for perfection. Thus they appear to us, but to him it was all in vain. Having understood that perfection could only exist in the spirit, in the idea, the moment it was transferred into matter — such as marble — he felt perfection slipping away from him. Its translation into matter was the most painful and yet necessary process.

To 'Night', the enchanting figure of a reclining woman abandoned in the oblivion of sleep, he made reference to in one of his Sonnets:

> *'Grato m'e 'l sonno, e piu l'esser di sasso*
> *Mentre che 'l danno e la vergogna dura;*
> *Non veder, non sentir m'e gran ventura:*
> *Però non mi destar, deh, parla basso!'*

(Dear to me is sleep and more being made of stone, Insensible of time's ignominies and injustices. Not to see, not to hear; these are my fastnesses. Therefore speak low, don't rouse me from my sleep).

The shame to which he refers is partly his own awareness of man's imperfection, not only in things great as man's struggle in front of creation, but even in things small as man's incapacity to run his own human affairs. The Florentines were going through a period of strong tyranny under the new Medici regime, reinstated with the help of the Pope. It was no more the liberal, patronizing leadership of Cosimo or even of the aristocratic Lorenzo, but the princely despotic rule of the Medici Dukes of Tuscany.

Michelangelo's struggle goes on but concerned with far more series matters. In 1436 he abandoned Florence, the statues of the Medici Tombs scattered all over the Sacristy of San Lorenzo, and never returned. One of his pupils had to arrange the Sacristy, and even finish some of the statues.

In Rome he was given new papal commissions like the architectural rearrangement of the Capitol Square and the model for Saint Peter's dome. Above all it was to the fresco on the huge wall behind the Altar of the Sistine Chapel, the Pope's private chapel that he entrusted his final message.

The 'Universal Judgement' is also Michelangelo's rejection of the harmonious, well ordered style which was the Renaissance, in favour of a composition which was far more emphatic and without consideration of arranged space or planes, foregrounds or backgrounds. It was the beginning of Baroque painting which took up Michelangelo's ideas nearly a century later.

In it the figure of Christ, colossal, high in the centre of the wall dominates the whole composition. Inscrutable, he is the Judge of the 'Dies Irae' and the souls abandon themselves to him with frantic exuberance. The artist seems to join them with the impetus of a new found faith. Perhaps in this moment, for the first time, Michelangelo found the answers he had been seeking. Thus he says in one of his last Sonnets:

> *'I can't not see anymore, your eternal light within all*
> *those who die, and with it not to feel of Thee desire'.*

RAFFAELLO SANZIO

The third great artist of the High Renaissance and in a way the greatest exponent of Renaissance ideals of form and content, is Raphael (1483-1520). Eight years younger than Michelangelo, the son of a painter from Urbino he was orphaned at the age of 11. Having already been initiated in the art of painting by an assistant of his father he later moved to Perugia where he became an apprentice to Perugino.

Raphael was the less original of the three artists. He was less genial than Leonardo and less intense than Michelangelo but the more humble and pleasant of the three. He, at least, always declared himself a painter and only a painter. Later he worked as an architect, town planner and archaeologist but these remained to him secondary activities.

At the beginning of his career he did not have a distinct style. In fact he went through various stilistique developments. Before the age of twenty, when apprenticed to Perugino, his youthful compositions are hardly distinguishable from those of his master. In 1501 when he moved to Florence, confronted with the art of Leonardo and Michelangelo, he revised his style.

It was in Florence that he started the series of paintings of the 'Virgin and Child' — an unsurpassable series of creations, each describing through the use of more and more perfect formal arrangements, the tender link between Mother and Child.

In the 'Tempi Madonna' (Ill.47), the tight way in which the mother and child interlock each other from the base up, starts with almost too strict a rhythm. However this is marvellously relaxed at the point when the two faces touch each other. Their two heads, profile to profile, seem to fill the canvas, sharing in the serenity of the sky immediately behind them.

This Madonna, in its pyramidal composition, is clearly inspired by Leonardo while its execution is definitely by Raphael's hand. The softness of the touch, the velvet smooth brush stroke, the lighter tones bringing out the most luminous effects endow the work with a lyrical note and a suavity typical of the Umbrian painters — the region where Urbino and Perugia are situated.

Less suave is the treatment of the group of portraits also painted in Florence before 1510 and which reveals in Raphael a new firmer grasp of human characters. Agnolo Doni (Ill.47) patron and friend of Raphael in Florence, is represented in a posture of elegant ease. His face reflects a sensitive and enlightened intelligence. His wife, Maddalena Doni (Ill.48), behind the exuberance of her generous figure, does not manage to conceal a certain hardness in the features of her face in spite of the hint of a smile. Their whole inner world can be seen in the understanding magnanimous look of Agnolo and the more guarded gaze of Maddalena. She seems apprehensive that the artist will paint her in her true light. The last two portraits in this volume (Ill. 49,50) are the two final masterpieces of Raphael's Florentine stay.

In 1508 the young artist reached Rome having been invited by Pope Julius II at the suggestion of Bramante, Raphael's compatriot from Urbino. His pleasant personality was immediately appreciated and liked in the Pope's entourage. Greatly impressed by the splendour of the Papal Court and the grandiosity of Rome which in those very years had taken away from Florence its role of artistic centre of Italy, Raphael went through a further development in his style. A new expressive power is now achieved by the artist, through a renovation of his own vocabulary of forms and a new chromatic scale.

In his paintings we find now an added sense of volume and mass ideal to render the engaging philosophical themes proposed by the Roman humanists for the Pope's apartments. In these years in fact Raphael is frescoing the Vatican rooms among which are the solemn scenes of the 'Disputation over the Sacrament' and 'The School of Athens'.

Form now becomes of even greater importance for our artist. It is solemn, grandiose, perfect. A form in itself so perfect as to identify completely with the subject it expresses. At this point Florentine painting developed into a model so admired and appreciated throughout Europe, that it became the inspiration to many a school of painting, the alphabet of western visual representation. In the divulgation of its achievements and aesthetic formulas, some saw it as a frozen model to copy and imitate.

Looking at the works of its real interpreters we know that it never could be captured in academic models, because the originals — even now — communicate life, render truth, suggest hope.

The classical world of the High Renaissance ended in a strange way. The art of Michelangelo and Raphael so dominated their contemporaries that it became their only model. In so doing, even their closer followers without realising it lost sight of the real content of their Masters.

Instead of imitating the reality surrounding them which was the starting point of all Renaissance artists in a certain style or 'manner', they imitated directly 'the manner' in which Michelangelo and Raphael had recreated it in their works. Thus the artistic production of this period came to be called 'Mannerist'. Its main exponents were the assistants of Raphael's Roman studio who had participated in his many fresco cycles and other papal commissions and had to complete some of his works after the artist's death in 1519.

The themes are still the ones used throughout the 15th and early 16th century — 'The Visitation,' episodes from the old Testament like 'the Daughters of Jethro', 'the Magdalene' or other biblical characters, portraits of important men and women. The latter now acquire a new significance because of their strange disinvolvement with the reality around them. Mannequins by the stilted poses, cold in the expression of their unemotional life, they still excite our admiration with their elegant demeanour, elaborate posture and sophisticated attires. They are represented in unreal spaces and circumstances, with unnatural colours. The colours are particularly divorced from nature, icy in their metallic tones, contrasting, clashing with each other.

In these paintings, outside time and space, there are no values or ideals to represent, no story or drama to live. They live only because of their aesthetic value and their formal expression. Should we then reject this style, ambiguous and disconcerting? But if it celebrates the triumph of the form, especially the human form, did not Leonardo, Michelangelo and Raphael lead us in its direction? Is it the ultimate expression of Renaissance art or its negations?

In Florence, however, Mannerism took the form of a far more lively and original artistic current, revalued by the art critics in recent years. It was there, partly due to the influence of artistic principles followed by Michelangelo in both his architecture and sculpture of the 1530's, that an anti-classical way of using the classical orders and other elements, led some artists to look at all classical principles in another way. Once again in Florence the artists were moving on, experimenting, trying new ways, drawing from one style its ultimate conclusions, while unconsciously laying down the foundations of the next one.

Jacopo Carrucci, called Pontormo, openly challenged the rules and compositions of the great masters by using them in an equivocal manner. (Ill. 52,53,54). His figures crowd the canvases in awkward uneasy groupings which deny space and classical harmony. On the whole it can be said that the human figure, but not nature, is still the centre of the artists' interest. Thus the characters in the pictures do not live in relation to the world around them, but in almost solitary existence enclosed within their ownselves.

Looking at some of the works of Pontormo or Rosso Fiorentino, his assistant, we see a series of human beings with dumb and distant expressions. As we look at them, their silence re-echoes in our hearts. To their drama we can find no response, we have no reaction. They appear like bodies without an inner substance, mannequins acting in a mock human comedy.

From 1545 on, Giorgio Vasari, the historian and architect to the Medici, utilized the whole repertory accumulated by the experience of the previous centuries in the commissions he executed for the Grand Dukes of Tuscany. Surrounded by a regiment of students, he decorated the walls of the Cinquecento Hall and the Grand Ducal apartments in the Palazzo Vecchio with a pictorial profusion in which an entire culture — literal, allegorical, historical — swarms in a figurative adaptation unredeemed by his most decorative subtlety. It is hard to extract moments of real artistic emotion from that raging illustrative rhapsody.

Yet precisely in this capacity to orchestrate multiple effects, the Florentine version of the 'manner' found one final grace. The last episode of the decoration is the frescoeing of the little Study of Francis I, with a series of mythological, classical and allegorical compositions. They had to be the pictorial fantasy of a visionary, which Francis I — continually lost in extravagant dreams, — certainly was.

Here in the compositions of Cavalori and Macchietti (Ill. 59,50,61), Mannerism loses in moments its arid pedantry in the felicity of a touch, of a fleeting heightening of fantasy. It is the last residue of the fading culture, the final meaning, the gracefulness to which the expression of form was reduced. This graceful rhythm was now to become the poetic discipline of all the arts throughout Europe, at least until the end of the century. A little while later, in Florence, the lyric drama was born.

BALDOVINETTI, ALESSIO, born Florence 1425, a pupil of Domenico Veneziano whose use of light and modelling he imitated; only a few works are securely attributed to him, a 'Sacra Conversazione' painted for the Medici, an 'Annunciation' now in the Uffizi and 'the Madonna' in the Louvre here reproduced. From 1450 he was the leading mosaicist of the Baptistery in Florence; died in his hometown in 1499.

BOTTICELLI, SANDRO, born Florence c. 1445, probably studied under Filippo Lippi and worked mainly on religious and mytholigical themes: 'The Birth of Venus' is one of his best-known works. He may have come under the influence of Savonarola who led a crusade against the 'abuses' of Renaissance Florence which included painting. After a period of prosperity, 1480-1500, his popularity greatly declined. Died 1510.

BRONZINO, ANGELO, born Florence 1503; greatly renowned in his lifetime as painter to the Medici and Consul of the Academy of Drawing; adopted son of Pontormo, his style was more elegant and refined with an undertone of great eroticism as can been seen in the 'Venus, Cupid, Folly and Time' in the National Gallery, London; his portraits, cold, cultured, unemotional are fascinating figure-representation; Eleonora da Toledo in the Wallace Collection, London and the Portrait of a Young Man of the Metropolitan Museum, New York are typical examples. Died Florence 1572.

MICHELANGELO BUONARROTI, born Caprese 1475 moving almost immediately to Florence; apprenticed to Ghirlandaio 1488 then transferred to the Medici school run by Bertoldo under the patronage of Lorenzo the Magnificent; went to Bologna in 1494 and to Rome in 1496 where he carved his 'Pieta' in St Peter's; he was in Florence in 1501-5 where he carved his 'David', summoned to Rome in 1505 to build a tomb for Pope Julius II but left after a quarrel; was again in Rome in 1508 working on the ceiling of the Sistine chapel; he was in Florence from 1524-34 to work on the Medici chapel but then settled finally in Rome where he remained until his death; between 1536 and 1541 he painted the 'Last Judgement' in the Sistine chapel but then became increasingly active as an architect, particularly as chief architect of St Peter's'; before his death in 1564 at the age of eighty-nine he carved three more 'Pietas'. Known as the 'divine Michelangelo' he was recognised as a genius in his own lifetime, a great poet and architect as well as painter, sculptor and draughtsman.

CARRUCCI JACOPO, called PONTORMO, born Florence 1494; a pupil of Andrea del Sarto, he later felt strongly the influence of Michelangelo's mature style; his major works include a lunette in the Medici villa of Poggio a Caiano illustrated here, a series of 'Passion Scenes' for the cloisters of the Certosa near Florence influenced by prints from Durer and a magnificent series of frescoes for S. ta Felicita, Florence, with the famous 'Depositions' and 'Annunciation'; here his style is powerful and disconcertingly original it initiates Mannerism as an independent and valid artistic current. Died Florence 1557.

CASTAGNO, ANDREA DEL, born Florence 1423, studied under Paolo Uccello and worked in Venice and Rome; painted magnificent passion scenes and 'The Last Supper' for the Church of S. Apollonia, now in the Castagno Museum; he painted famous frescoes of Men and Women now also in the Castagno Museum and the equestrian portrait of 'Niccolo da Tolentino' in the Cathedral of Florence; imitated both Masaccio and Donatello last manner with vigour and vitality; died Florence 1457.

DONATELLO, DONATO DI NICCOLÓ, born Florence 1386 and apprenticed as a sculptor to Ghiberti; working on the Baptistery doors 1403 and in Florence cathedral from 1406; produced works in partnership with the sculptor Michelozzo from c. 1425; visited Rome 1401-3, Padua 1443-53. The most influential individual artist of the fifteenth century, he revolutionised sculpture, moving in his own work from the purest classical style to the very powerful dramatic sculptures of his later years. The bronze 'David' is an illustration of his classical period and the wood 'Mary Magdalene' the masterpiece of his later work. Died 1466.

DOMENICO DI TOMMASO BIGORDI, called GHIRLANDAIO, born Florence 1445, the son of a goldsmith was an apprentice to Baldovinetti but retained the fine exact sense of line of the goldsmiths; painted in the Sistine Chapel 'Christ Calling the First Apostles' with vivid realism; his most important work was the frescoes for Santa Maria Novella of 'Scenes from the Life of the Virgin and St. John the Baptist' — good craftsmanship and down to earth; Michelangelo was an apprentice with him for two years and derived from him the sound teaching of his fresco technique; died Florence 1494.

GIOVANNI DA FIESOLE, called FRA' ANGELICO, born in Vicchio near Fiesole 1387 the major part of his work is to be found in the series of frescoes for the Convent of San Marco, Florence. His last fresco work, the decoration of Nicolas V Chapel in the Vatican reach a higher sense of composition; many of his altarpieces and religious panels of exquisite craftmanship and inspirations are to be found in the main European museums; blessed by the church before his death in Rome in 1455, the recognition came for his holy life as well as for his inspired works of art.

GIOTTO DI BONDONE, born Florence c.1266, probably a pupil of Cimabue; joined painters' guild 1311; was court painter to Robert of Anjou 1329-33 and overseer of work on Florence cathedral 1334; worked for Visconti in Milan; 1335-6. Particularly noted for his frescoes and the humanity of his figures, the 'Life of St. Francis' in Assisi (though disputed) 1297-1305 and the 'Lives of the Virgin and Christ completed c.1303 in the Arena chapel Padua, are among his most famous works. Died 1377.

BENOZZO DI LESE, called BENOZZO GOZZOLI, born Florence 1420, a disciple of Beato Angelio famous for his two fresco cycles in the Medici Chapel, Florence and in the Cemetery, Pisa which both linger in the detailing of contemporary Florentine life, rich with portraits of well known Florentines; great effervescence of colour and decorative elements; died in Pisa 1479.

LEONARDO DA VINCI, born Vinci 1452, trained as a painter under Verrocchio and entered painters' guild 1472; went to Milan 1382, working for Lodovico Sforza, where he painted the 'Last Supper' 1497 and 'The Virgin and Child with St. Anne and St John'; returned to Florence 1500 when the French invaded Milan; worked for Cesare Borgia as a military engineer 1502-3; returned to Milan in 1506 and was made painter and engineer to Francis I of France 1507; went to Rome 1513-16 to seek, though unsuccessfully, the pope's favour and left Italy for France 1517. Leonardo was universally gifted as inventor, scientist, architect, musician, mathematician as well as being a painter and superb draughtsman. Died 1519.

LIPPI, FILIPPINO, born Florence 1457, son of Filippi; a pupil of Fra' Diamante and later Botticelli whose style he closely follows; the Angel Adoring and the Madonna with SS. Jerome and Dominic, National Gallery London are typical examples of his early style; best work 'Vision of St. Bernard' in the badia, Florence (1486) pervaded of a poetical, if overacted, lyricism; later fresco works in Rome and Florence intensely dramatic and picturesque, anticipate mannerism; completed Masaccio's frescoes in the Brancacci Chapel;

LIPPI, FRA' FILIPPO, born Florence 1406, Carmelite monk living in the Convent of S.ta Maria de Carmine; first fresco for that church 'The Relaxation of the Carmelite Rule' (1432); initial work on the imitation of Masaccio with interest in volume and perspective; good examples 'Tarquinia Madonna' in the Brera, Milan and 'The Annunciation' in S. Lorenzo, Florence; moved to a more gothic decorative style in the 'Scenes from the Lives of SS. Stephen and John the Baptist' in Prato Cathedral (1452-1465); will be one of the strongest influences on the 19th century Pre-Raphaelites. Both his decorative linearism and the deep humanity of his figures will be inherited by Botticelli; died Florence 1469.

MASACCIO, TOMMASO DI GIOVANNI, born Florence 1401, entered painters' guild 1422; worked on his greatest paintings, the fresco of the 'Trinity' in Santa Maria Novella, Florence, and those in the Brancacci chapel, Florence between 1425 and his death in 1428 when only twenty-seven.

MASOLINO DA PANICALE, born 1383 in unknown locality; worked in Florence in the Gothic style until his association with Masaccio brought him closer to Renaissance manners; together they painted 'Virgin with St. Anne' in the Uffizi and the frescoes of 'Miracles and Life of Christ and St. Peter' in S.ta Maria del Carmine, Florence; painted a triptych for S.ta Maria Maggiore, Rome 'the Miracle of the Snow' and frescoes for S. Clemente, Rome; in the frescoes for Castiglion d'Olona, Como, reverted to charming gothic fairy tale manner; twice in Hungary painting for Matthias Corvinus; last documented 1447.

PIERO DELLA FRANCESCA, born Borgo San Sepolcro in Umbria c.1410; studied in Florence and worked independently in Borgo, Rimini, Ferrara, Arezzo, Rome and Urbino; town councillor in Borgo 1442; stopped painting in the 1470's perhaps to concentrate on mathematics. One of his most famous works is the fresco depicting the story of the Cross which he began in Arezzo 1452. Died 1492.

PIERO DI COSIMO, born Florence 1461; a pupil of Cosimo Rosselli and Signorelli; painted religious works under Signorelli and Leonardo's influence — also bizarre mythological fantasies like 'the Discovery of Honey' in Worcester, Mass. and 'the Discovery of Wine' in the Fogg Museum, Mass; interesting his 'Hunting Scene' of the Metropolitan, New York and 'the Battle of the Lapiths and Centaurs' of the National Gallery, London; most poetical 'the Death of Procris' of the same Museum; died Florence 1521.

RAPHAEL (RAFFAELLO SANZIO), born Urbino 1483, the son of a painter; studied under Perugino and then went to Florence where he absorbed the teachings of Leonardo and Michelangelo; summoned to Rome by Pope Julius II 1508 to work on the decoration of the papal apartments in the Vatican which are his greatest achievement; while in Rome he painted the altarpieces the 'Sistine Madonna' 1512 and the 'Transfiguration' 1520, succeeded Bramante as architect of St Peter's 1514 and became superintendent of the streets of Rome, responsible for all town planning 1517. Died 1520.

ROSSO FIORENTINO, GIOVANNI BATTISTA, born 1494; active Florence 1513-1523; formally bold and intensely dramatic his Italian works developed Mannerist style; Francis I invited him to France with Primaticcio where they initiated the Mannerist School of Fontainebleau; last documented 1540.

UCCELLO, PAOLO, born Pratovecchio near Florence 1397; started as mosaicist in Florence Baptistery and in Venice Cathedral; returned to Florence 1430 developed interest in geometry and perspective; interesting perspectival effects in fresco of 'the Flood' in S.ta Maria Novella, Florence; three panels of the Rout of San Romano' in London, Paris and Florence are his major works; perspective effects here deny space but boldly bring out impact of the fight; died Florence 1475.

VENEZIANO, DOMENICO. Perhaps of Venetian origin, settled in Florence in 1420's; previously worked with Pisanello, the international gothic painter and in Florence with Paolo Uccello; his Scenes from the Life of the Virgin in S. Egidio, Florence, have not survived but Piero della Francesca worked to these with Domenico; Vasari mentions Veneziano use of oil painting which he introduced to Florence, perhaps untrue, but Veneziano's use of colour and light in compositions were very influential for Florentine painters; major works 'Carnesecchi Madonna and two Saints' in the National Gallery, London (1440) and 'St. Lucy's Altarpiece' in the Uffizi, Florence; died Florence 1461.

1 – GIOTTO

Stories from the Life of St Francis of Assisi, detail
Bardi Chapel, Church of S. ta Croce — Florence

Giotto painted two fresco cycles of the Life of St. Francis of Assisi. The first, one in the Upper Church of S. Francesco in Assisi, was executed before 1305, and the second, shown here, in Florence between the years 1317 and 1325. Often the same scene is represented in both cycles. It is therefore particularly interesting to compare the artist's stylistic development through them.

As Vasari, the Renaissance historian wrote in his Life of Giotto: 'He alone, although born amidst incompetent artists...succeeded in resuscitating art and restoring her to a path that may be called the true one.' Vasari was referring to Giotto's extraordinary involvement with true human situations and his ability to bring out the relevant elements, discarding all superfluous or purely decorative ones.

Giotto's realistic, direct method of narration is most evident in this scene of Francis' rejection of his father and all material comforts. The Franciscan story relates how the young Francis answered his father, who had threatened to disinherit him, by baring himself even of his own tunic.

In this scene, the angry humiliated father, holding his son's tunic, is pulled back by his friends; while Francis, covered by a simple loin cloth, points in the direction of the 'riches' he will be seeking from now on. The plain wall behind them seems to give solemnity to the scene. The boldly outlined figures of father and son stand out, silhouetted against such an ideal background. Notice the warm tonality of most of the composition in vibrant terracottas, pinks and ivories, contrasted only by the soft azure of the sky.

2 – GIOTTO

Story from the Life of St Francis of Assisi, detail
Bardi Chapel, Church of S. ta Croce — Florence

This detail comes from the same fresco cycle of illustration No. 1. According to a Franciscan legend, at the moment of his death, St. Francis is supposed to have appeared to brother Augustin and to the Bishop Guido of Assisi. Both were lying ill in different places and both died at the same time, calling to the Saint 'Wait for me. I am coming.'

In this detail, a Franciscan monk sitting at the feet of the Bishop's bed has fallen asleep, exhausted by the long protracted vigil. Giotto draws with such vigour and so few lines the face of the sleeping young man we almost feel the weight of his head as it rests more and more heavily on his supporting hand.

On one or two scratches on the brother's shoulder one can follow the process used in the fresco technique. These frescoes, very damaged and repeatedly restored, have become in places rather bare. In this technique, a fresh layer of plaster was applied to a wall, whose surface had been particularly roughed in order for the plaster to adhere perfectly to it. The fresh layer of plaster had to be painted over before it dried — about one working day.

The fresco painter consequently had to use a lot of improvisation whenever the prepared drawings, transferred on the wall, did not tally with the ones of the previous day. A bold and inventive artist like Giotto would come out at his best in such working conditions.

3 — TOMMASO DI SER GIOVANNI, called MASACCIO
Crucifixion
Museum of Capodimonte — Naples

Few paintings exist by Masaccio and the earliest surviving one is dated not earlier than 1422. We know therefore very little about the artist's possible apprenticeship to another painter, perhaps in Florence, where he came at the age of 16-17.

One of his first and best known works is the Pisa Poliptych. Made up of many panels, these are now dispersed among many European museums. In the 'Madonna and Child' with angels in the National Gallery, London, the main panel of the poliptych, the artist's derivation from Giotto and his awareness of the problems of consistent lighting from one direction and of space rendering are evident.

The panel illustrated here is part of the same poliptych, and even within the traditional iconography of a medieval crucifixion — where Christ on the cross on a mountain top and the Maries at his feet, are set against a gold ground — demonstrates the artists conscious manipulation of light and of human feelings. Christ on the cross suffers more as a man than as a God. Even with all his resignation, the physical tension of the arm muscles, the stretched ribs on which the head sinks are painfully emphasised by the stark light which shines on them. The Virgin, simple and humane, seems to hide in her blue cloak, not only her figure, but her grief, which like a mounting tide seems to swell inside her. Marta with a most sensitive expression maintains a silence far too eloquent. The Magdalene, a cascade of gold and fiery reds, as she falls to her knees, seems to invade our own ground with her tunic spilling over the edge of the picture. The figure of the Magdalene was inserted by the artist at a later stage as can be seen by her halo, superimposed on the ground with a thin layer of paint, not beaten into a pattern as the other three.

4 — TOMMASO DI SER GIOVANNI, called MASACCIO
The Expulsion of Adam and Eve from Paradise
Brancacci Chapel, Church of the Carmine — Florence

The series of frescoes of the Life and Miracles of Christ and the Apostles in the Brancacci Chapel are perhaps Masaccio's greatest contribution to Renaissance art.

The cycle was executed in collaboration with Masolino between 1425 — 1427 and was later finished by Filippino Lippi. Masaccio's scenes 'The Expulsion of Adam and Eve', 'The Tribute Money', 'The Baptism of the Neophites', 'St. Peter curing the Sick with his Shadow' and 'The Death of Ananias' are by far the most important. All through the 15th century these compositions inspired the Florentine artists and were considered by Michelangelo 'the school of the Renaissance artists'.

In the fresco of Adam and Eve's Expulsion from Paradise, the first of the frescoes in order of appearance, we find for the first time the stark human body used as a vehicle to describe human emotions: the shame in Adam, the despair in Eve for what she has lost for herself and her companion. A careful observation of the human anatomy is evident in the contracted muscles of the stomach and the bulging torso of Adam or in the slack posture of Eve's body expanded in the utterance of her cry. In the abject shame of Adam's sorrow, in the animal wail of Eve, Masaccio pours all the sorrow that humanity will feel for that exodus which will never cease as long as mankind will tread the earth.

The fresco of the Trinity was painted in the years 1427-28, before Masaccio's fatal journey to Rome. Reported in a late 15th century chronicle it ended tragically with the death of the artist. As the chronicler said 'He died in Rome of poison aged 26. He was greatly loved by Ser Brunellesco who taught him many things. When the above said Filippo heard of his death, he was very upset and used to say to his domestics 'we have had a great loss'.

Indeed Brunelleschi had taught many things to Masaccio and above all he must have shared with him his studies on perspective. The fresco of the Trinity, whose detail of the Virgin is illustrated here, when seen in its entirety represents a church chapel, barrel vaulted and framed by a perfectly rounded Brunelleschian arch with Doryc columns set within two corynthian pilasters and a classical entablature. Inside this chapel, Christ on the cross appears with God and the Dove just above his head. This apparition is silently witnessed by two donors, devoutly kneeling on the very foreground, outside the chapel's space. Their lifelike size gives the whole scene a human scale which involves us more directly in the religious event.

The Virgin, as it appears in our illustration, looks straight outside the picture pointing to her son's death. Executed with extreme sobriety of colour and expression, only her unfocusing eyes and the tight lips, are evidence of her grief.

The Trinity is Masaccio's masterpiece of perspective effects and bold foreshortenings. As one walks in front of the flat wall on which it is painted, it is hard to believe that the chapel is not there in three dimension and that we cannot actually walk right inside it.

6 – MASOLINO DA PANICALE
S. Catherine of Alexandria
Church of S. Clemente al Celio — Rome

This fresco is part of a cycle on the Life of Saint Catherine which the artist painted in Rome around 1428 in collaboration with Masaccio. Masolino's interest in spatial effects within a well structured perspectival scheme is evidence of Masaccio's influence on his work at the time.

His true inspiration however, comes out the moment he abandons himself to the lyrical sinuous line with which he paints the weightless figure of the Saint. The whole picture in fact appears to concentrate and gather momentum around the blonde spiritual figure of Catherine, whose delicate complexion is brought out by the lapis-lazuli blue of the background.

Gothic sentiment and Renaissance structures make of this picture a rare witness of the co-existence in Florence at the time of the two styles.

43

7 – MASOLINO DA PANICALE
Herod's Banquet, detail
Baptistery — Castiglion D'Olona, near Como

Masolino lived a very varied life, moving between Italy and Hungary where he worked for Mathias Corvino, its enlightened King. This may be one of the reasons why he worked so often in collaboration with Masaccio, who it seems, at least for the Brancacci chapel, was called in to finish the series abandoned by Masolino on his way to Hungary. Later they again worked together in Rome, exposing Masolino twice to the volumetric, more realistic and weighty manner of Masaccio. We have already seen the latter's influence on Masolino's perspective and structures. Later in his life, however, after Masaccio's death, Masolino reverted to his more decorative and linear, international gothic style.

In the fresco executed for the Baptistery of Castiglion D'Olona we see in the detail of the Salome, halfway through her convincing persuasive dance to obtain from Herod the head of the Baptist, a most exquisite use of the decorative subtlety of the international gothic. Salome, contained within various shades of green, musky on the architectures, intense and gem like in the background, the form of her body underlined by the dark gripping tunic, stands out in the subtle luminosity of her beautiful face and white blonde hair. Poised, she darts a meaningful glance to assess psychologically her effect on the king; however Masaccio's lesson appears again in the volumetric rendering of the face by the use of a well planned, consistent light.

8 – FRA GIOVANNI DA FIESOLE, called FRA ANGELICO
The Crib
Town Museum — Forlì

Fra Giovanni da Fiesole spent his life celebrating and diffusing the gospel through his paintings. Siding with the renewed fervour of the Dominican movement, which during the 15th century in Florence under the direction of Fra Dominici was preaching a more intense and innocent belief in the Christian doctrine, the Friar used his brush to preach in the best way he knew. This is perhaps what Ruskin meant when he wrote 'Angelico is not an artist properly so-called, but an inspired saint'. While recognising the religious involvement of the man, Ruskin failed to understand that he was also a great artist.

This small panel discovered only during the last century and not documented, can be safely attributed to our artist, as most of the critics have done. Its lyrical quality is derived by the sincere handling and total absorption of the artist in the subject. No elements detract from the simple narration of the main event, even the singing angels are kept in a low key, not to interrupt the Virgin and St. Jospeh's first adoration of their own baby. The ass and the oxen, even they on their knees, emanate a warmth which is expressed in terms of light. This same light inundates and radiates back from the baby who revels in it.

The story is simple, the structure which contains it is humble but it is perfectly adequate to house the two holy figures, baby, oxen and ass. The axis of St Joseph and Mary placed as they are, at opposite angles, accentuate the space of the foreground. The angels' golden haloes, standing out against the sombre profile of the mountains at night, are in turn picked out in the golden halo of the moon which seems to conceal the stretched hand of God pointing to his son.

9 – FRA GIOVANNI DA FIESOLE, called FRA ANGELICO

Universal Judgement, detail
Museum of San Marco — Florence

This is a detail of Angelico's grandiose composition of the Universal Judgement. It is one of the first Renaissance works to represent and conceive space on a grand scale. It is vast, physical as well as conceptual, which includes human and holy beings, angels and demons, the damned and the elected. Here we find Fra Giovanni not only as the religious man but as an original up to date artist.

The iconography of the Judgement may have as a precedent the well known judgement of Hieronimus Bosch, especially with regard to the groups of sinners and damned on the right hand side — not included in this detail. However, Angelico completely conquers all past iconographies the moment he opens his scene with a bold central one-point-perspective to the vast emptiness of a sidereal firmament. In our detail the good, holy characters are naîvely confronted with the bad and the damned. Their grimaces, as in a mystery play — the religious plays often enacted in churches during particular religious events — overact their distress, repentance or anger.

It is interesting to notice the man in the pink tunic on the right, wearing what seems very much like a monk's habit. Here perhaps the artist is warning his confraternity that wearing such a habit is no assurance of Paradise.

The panel dated around 1431 was one of the first works of the artist's maturity. The strange frame which contains it is shaped like a long rectangle, topped in the centre by three circles. The middle one, the tallest, contains Christ enthroned surrounded by angels whose trumpets we just see in our detail. The whole panel was meant to act as an elevated Choir Stalls' back, used for the High Sung Masses. The orchestration and polyphony of the colours and forms of Beato Angelico must have come in full play under the thousand torches and evaporating incense used in such ceremonies.

10 – FRA GIOVANNI DA FIESOLE, called FRA ANGELICO
San Marco's Altarpiece, detail
Museum of San Marco — Florence

The San Marco's Altarpiece, the most solemn and complex of the 'Sacre Conversazioni' composition of all the 15th century, is Angelico's masterpiece. Painted between 1438 and 1440, around the Madonna and Child enthroned, a group of eight Saints, three of them Dominicans — the order which Fra Angelico belonged to — are holding what is called a 'sacred conversation'. Angels just behind the throne, at either side, are against a background wall which separates the composition from a most verdent hilly, wooded ground. He creates great harmony between the formal order of creation — magnificently structured in the background with a series of strong scenario — like pines — and the human world in the foreground enriched by the strong visual patterns and textures of the carpet in our illustration — the composition culminates in the plain gold ground of the small crucifixion panel of gothic derivation.

Here most of the iconographic elements already found in Masaccio's Deposition confirm the advanced realism of Masaccio. In this work, Angelico is bringing in different artistic expressions, different styles, all linked by their common subject matter. Christ's crucifixion is obviously the subject of that hieratic conversation that a group of Saints, looking more like Doctors of the Church or humanistic scholars, are holding around the holy Virgin.

11 – FRA GIOVANNI DA FIESOLE, called FRA ANGELICO
The Deposition
Museum of San Marco — Florence

This painting, the central part of a large altarpiece, was commissioned around 1418-20 to Lorenzo Monaco by the Strozzi family for the Church of S.ta Trinita in Florence. Lorenzo, the great master of the international gothic, only painted three small portions above the frame of this panel: 'The Noli Me Tangere', 'The Resurrection' and 'The Holy Women' while the main panel and the predella were painted 20 years later by Fra Angelico.

Here our artist must not have felt inhibited by the gothic arches of the frame surrounding his panel. The composition is the first in which Angelico shows a real Renaissance understanding of space and classical rendering in the weighty representation of the characters. With their long gravely pleated tunics, they offer a series of vertical lines continued by the cross and counteracted by the steps of the ladder on which the dead body of Jesus is eased down from. This prevalence of horizontal and verticals gives a new stability and calm to the composition new to the gothic traditional handling of the theme.

Only in the group of the holy women on the left of the cross is there perhaps a remnant of gothic crowding and in the choice of buildings in the background, castles and walled town; the architecture of the past century is very much in evidence. The buildings of Michelozzo, the architect chosen by Cosimo de Medici to rebuild the Convent of San Marco and who had just finished the castle of Trebbio — which can be recognised as the castle at the left of the crucifixion can also be identified here. Michelozzo himself appears as the man in the black hood, standing on the ladder just under Christ's lifted arm.

It seems that Angelico copied other characters from life in this work; most interesting is the portrait of a member of the Strozzi family who commissioned the work, recognisable as the man in the red turban at the right of Christ.

12 – FRA GIOVANNI DA FIESOLE, called FRA ANGELICO
The Deposition, detail
Museum of San Marco — Florence

Having already stressed the gothic character of the building at the back of the Deposition, it is interesting to notice in the detail, Angelico's construction of his background. The strongly diminished size of the buildings outside the town walls gives an impression of great distance from the panel's foreground. The town itself, seemingly toy like and filled with very simple cubic structures, represents very much a typical Italian town around the beginning of the century. Florence, like Pisa and Siena were all enclosed within walls very much like the one painted here and thus constricted for space, the buildings were crowded in a manner similar to what we see.

Each house owner, not able to expand any other way, would keep building storey over storey on their house, thus robbing his neighbour of light and air, or forcing him to raise his own building. Laws were passed by the end of the 14th century to refrain from this habit. Only during the 15th century, buildings were pulled down and space created for squares and gardens. This we see reflected in later Renaissance paintings.

The castle which one can see commanding the highest spot in the town has been identified as the Castle of Giovanni Acuto, Sir John Hawkwood, in Montecchio. Sir John was a famous English soldier whose equestrian portrait was painted by Paolo Uccello on one of the walls of Florence Cathedral. The works remains to this day one of the masterpieces of early Italian Renaissance portraiture.

13 – FRA GIOVANNI DA FIESOLE, called FRA ANGELICO
The Mocking of Christ, detail
Museum of San Marco — Florence

In 1436 Pope Eugenio IV gave the Convent of San Marco to the Dominican Friars of Fiesole. This was Friar Giovanni's community, a vigorous branch of the learned order, under the particular guidance of the Beato Dominici, a reformer and a man of great moral force and integrity.

From 1437 until 1452 Cosimo de Medici entrusted the rebuilding of the old Convent to the architect Michelozzo, while the Dominicans asked their own brother GIOVANNI to execute the fresco decorations. Angelico, undoubtedly with the help of some assistants, planned and painted a series of scenes from the Life of Christ in the corridors and the friars' cells on the first floor, ending with an imposing scene of the Crucifixion in the Chapter House.

Over 35 of the frescoes are securely attributed to him. The scenes are truly magnificent and the most pure and poetical part of Angelico's oeuvre. Story after story of the Annunication, the Adoration, the Noli Me Tangere, Crucifixion, Resurrection, Crowning of the Virgin, etc. both human and celestial biblical events unfold under a narration which is at the same time simple and effective in the essentiality of the elements chosen.

This mocking of Christ is a perfect example of them in the reduction of the story to its essentials: one mocker, one God, a few hands ready to hit, more often missing. It is in the spiritual and yet volumetric rendering of Christ in the white robe, in the bold foreshortening of the wooden box on which he is seated, slanted at an angle almost projecting him onto the onlooker's plane, that Angelico's direct language can best be heard.

14 – FRA GIOVANNI DA FIESOLE, called FRA ANGELICO
The Prayer in the Garden
Museum of San Marco — Florence

The Prayer is part of a series of 36 panels which, originally assembled together, covered a sideboard which contained the most valuable silver ex-votos of the Church of the Santissima Annunziata in Florence.

Perhaps commissioned by Piero de Medici in 1448, the sideboard was soon removed from its original location and the panels were dissembled in 1782. The critics, who have recognised the extreme quality and the autography of most of the panels, have recently reconstructed their probable arrangement and reorganized the order of execution of the parts.

Once again the subjects are stories from the Life of Jesus, treated with a sophistication and spatial understanding which points to great maturity on behalf of the artist.

Angelico reaches here a climax in his own artistic experience. His rendering of space, which reminds us of Giotto, although rendered in a simple form is well structured. The foreground, spacious and well developed and the sudden diminution of size of the middle ground where Jesus prays, points to the use of psychological effects. It is like the diction used in a child's story, when the voice changes with the qualities of the characters described. Within the ample spaces suggested, each man appears isolated by his own contour. The trees live in isolation, the flowers can be counted each one separately. In this way the artist tries to express that feeling of utter solitude which Christ felt during that endless night when he kept awakening his diciples begging them in vain not to fall asleep. A light coming from the left hand side announces the arrival of dawn, illuminating in its own trail Jesus' shoulders, the trees and the angel who turns into a pool of gold.

APPARVIT AT̃ EI ANGELVS DECEE CONFORTANS EVM. LVCE. XXII . C.

59

15 — FRA FILIPPO LIPPI
Madonna and Child
Palazzo Medici Riccardi — Florence

Filippo Lippi in this Madonna painted for the Medici family, a work of his middle period, demonstrates his real understanding of Renaissance volumetry and space.

The division of the panel within its shallow space into three clear zones, the foreground marked by the marble parapet, the space occupied by the Virgin who is slightly advanced in her seated position from the niche, and the hollow created by the well recessed cavity of the niche itself are most convincing. The artist nonetheless revalues each surface, by the use of patterns — variegated marble panels, brocade and pleated draperies of the Virgin's dress, sculptorial details in the architecture, accentuated filigree pattern on the halo — so that no element becomes secondary because of its recession into space.

By these devices Lippi reacts to the Renaissance emphasis on three dimensionality, feeling perhaps that this might have turned the art of painting into a poor imitation of sculpture, instead of exploiting, at the fullest, the qualities inherent to painting on one definite surface. His lesson will be fully absorbed by Botticelli. In the round bulging forms of the baby however, Lippi does not forget the lesson of Masaccio and of the new realism of the Renaissance.

61

16 – FRA FILIPPO LIPPI
Herod's Banquet, detail
Prato Cathedral — Prato

The frescoes executed for the Cathedral of Prato between 1452 and 1464 show the artist's work in its fullest and richest phase. Having absorbed all the lessons in space and perspective from the great Renaissance masters Brunelleschi, Masaccio and Albert having experimented in bringing these together with renewed values of surface and line, in Prato the artist is finally free to develop a rich and ever varying narrative style.

In this scene of Salome's dance, given the ample area of the marble floor, arranged with well pronounced lines all merging — if extended — on one common focal point, given the set planes of the table and wall in the middleground and the distant hills in the background, the dance is about to take place. And it is in the continuous alternation of light and shade, of changing poses and varied expressions, of musical cadences and sudden changes of direction that Botticelli finds its truest artistic expression.

Looking at Salome we see her softly swaying on one side of the chequered hall on the point to start another pirouette. In her delicate sensitive features can be seen her compenetration with her grave deed. At the centre of the room, tapping on the table at her daughter's macabre rhythm, Erodiade, romantically bathed, in light suffers no repentance.

17 – FRA FILIPPO LIPPI
Funerals of St. Steven
Prato Cathedral — Prato

This scene, from the same cycle as the previous one (Ill. N.16), shows a magnificent Brunelleschian type of setting. In the church perhaps inspired from Brunelleschi's San Lorenzo in Florence, the carefully rendered architectural details lead the eye with great expertise right to the focal point of the composition.

While looking towards the central point, all the characters in the scene arrange themselves neatly, in what at first appear well ordered ranks. Looking a little closer each character has a different expression, a different reaction, as they are variously affected by the holy man's death.

St. Steven himself, the only powerful horizontal to counteract so many vertical and orthogonal lines, steadies the whole composition, while his rigid paleness stresses the peace and quiet reached in death.

18 – ANDREA DEL CASTAGNO
The Last Supper
S. Apollonia — Florence

Andrea, a pupil of Paolo Uccello, worked at first in Venice at some fescoes for the absid of the old Church of San Zaccaria. He appears to be influenced both by Masaccio's bold sense of volume and by Donatello's love of movement and the rendering of nervous energy. His interest however, since quite early in his career, will centre more and more in the energetic rendering of the human figure through the appropriate use of light, itself a source of energy.

In the frescoes which he started in 1445 for the Refectory of the Church of S. Apollonia in Florence, he demonstrates also his concern to experiment with the rendering of hard, shiny surfaces. In a way this is another aspect of the same phenomenon since such surfaces are the best vehicle for the reflection or intensification of light.

In the last supper we see a series of planes, hard and linear, like the white starched cloth of the Apostle's table, the wall panels of variegated marble each with a different power of reflecting light, almost squeezing the apostles between them. Jesus, in the very foreground, appears to stand alone and still, almost frozen in the realisation of the 'betrayal' — But what links the various characters to one another is their being invested by the light, that seems to keep them within a tight grip. Their own flesh seems hardly softer than the marble against which they are silhouetted.

19 – ANDREA DEL CASTAGNO
The Last Supper, detail
S. Apollonia — Florence

The central part of the fresco already discussed (Ill. N.18) appears in close up even harsher than it does when seen from the distance. Furthermore the little space suggested from afar, dissolves the moment we come closer. This is supposedly meant by the artist to express the close association between the sitters, almost their inevitable coming together.

In Castagno's world of hard surfaces, even the halo, symbol of the gold light of revelation, solidifies into one disc of hard metal. We can almost hear the clash of Christ's fingers coming into contact with it in the act of blessing St. John.

Christ's profile exaggeratedly indented vies in firmness with the lines of the wall panels, a chromatic contrast accentuates their diversity. The series of patterns, the small checks of the table cloth, the draped cloth against the back of the Apostle's seat and the skilful rendering of each surface, in other words Andrea's ultimate conquest of the rendering of different tactile sensations, will be imitated and applied by many later Renaissance painters.

20 – ANDREA DEL CASTAGNO
The Cumaean Sibyl
Castagno Museum, Castagno — Florence

In a series of frescoes of 'Famous Men and Women' which he painted for the Church of St. Apollonia, Florence, after 1450, Castagno has created the prototypes of an idealized, heroic humanity.

As lasting and as splendid as the iridescent marble surfaces against which they appear, Castagno's characters have the nobility and the strength of their creator's artistic convictions.

The Cumaean sibyl, tight lipped, mysterious and precious as the riddles through which she expressed her prophecies, is the predecessor of Michelangelo's Sistine sibyls. Her elongated sensuous neckline, her perfect oval face, her refined features speak the language of intellect and spiritual refinement achieved by the artist with his incisive line and fine draughtsmanship.

21 – ANDREA DEL CASTAGNO

Eve

Villa Pandolfini, Legnaia — Florence

In another fresco cycle for Villa Pandolfini we recognize Eve, the progenitor of mankind.

Primitive and wild, she appears magnificently portrayed in her sturdy figure, the woman who — to satisfy her sensuality — had to bear first the weight of God's curse: "I will greatly multiply thy sorrow and thy conception; in sorrow thou shalt bring forth children." (Gen. 3.16).

She holds a spindle, symbol of the labour which she has to share with Adam to secure their livelihood on this earth. She appears as durable as the granite behind her, able to stand up to her hard destiny. Andrea has expressed in her face experience and determination in a representation which, for the first time in the history of art, rehabilitates Eve and, through her, the whole of mankind.

22 – PAOLO UCCELLO
The Profanation of the Host, detail
National Gallery of the Marche — Urbino

During his youth Paolo Uccello must have been influenced by international gothic sources, perhaps in the works of Gentile da Fabriano and of Lorenzo Monaco, both present in Florence in the 1420's.

His love for the mysterious and almost the metaphysical, evident in his handling of colour and of subject matter — think of the Rout of San Romano in the National Gallery — points to his sources being more genuinely unrealistic than anything he could have found in Florence.

Between 1425 and 1430 the artist was working in Venice as a mosaicist at San Marco. There he must have been greatly attracted by the decoration of Gentile da Fabriano and Pisanello on the walls of the Ducal Palace. Those frescoes, now destroyed, with their scenes of violent storms and battles, must have deeply impressed the young Uccello. They can certainly give us a clue to his famous horses — grey, red and black — appearing in this panel, even though in a very subdued form and which, in the daring foreshortenings of the Rout of San Romano, send us straight back to Pisanello.

The theme of this scene, one of six parts of a predella, illustrates a medieval legend. According to this a woman was induced by a merchant to sell him a consecrated host, which, to insult it, he threw into the fire. The Host bled and the blood ran out into the street making people run to see what was the matter. Consequently the woman was sentenced to be hanged. In the next illustration she is shown dead with an angel and a devil contending for her soul.

Something of the medieval flavour of the story may have been purposefully maintained in Uccello's composition. The simplified hilly landscape, the expressionistic colours. Nonetheless there is something extremely audacious in the choice of those very colours, while the physical types, their careful modelling, the use of direct lighting manifest his involvement with renaissance techniques and solutions.

23 – PAOLO UCCELLO

The Profanation of the Host, detail
National Gallery of the Marche — Urbino

In this final panel of the Predella with the story of the Profanation of the Host (See also Ill. N.22) the taut stretch of the bier with the body of the dead sinner almost exemplifies what is happening. Two devils and two angels are contending with her body. The contrast between the two groups — the blue and gold skeleton-like figures of the devils and the rounded soft figure of the angels — is re-echoed in the black base and red stretcher above. The whole painting furthermore is divided between foreground, organised and firmly structured with a series of horizontals and verticals and the soft curving background with its undulating hills and sloping horizon.

The colours and patterns are so cleverly construed as to turn the picture into a delightful visual experience. Notice the way the gilt devil and his patterned skeleton is re-echoed in the gold and black pattern of the altar front panel, or the blue devil stretching at the feet of the woman's body starts a pattern of blues and reds continued at the end of the bier in the red and blue wings of the angels.

24 – DOMENICO VENEZIANO
Adoration of the Kings
Staatliche Museen — Berlin

Little is known of Domenico's origins and apprenticeship during his early years, except that it appears that he originated from Venice.

The work shown here is attributed to our artist by all the critics, alas without any documentation. It belongs to the earlier part of Veneziano's career. Although discovered in Florence, it must have been painted before his exposure to Florentine Renaissance Art. In this magnificent royal procession of monumental horses and decorative knights which file through the open expanse of countryside receding in the distance — among the mountains — to the far-off waters of Lake Garda, we can see the chromatic splendour of Pisanello modulated by the use of infinite, luminous space. Not quite the perspective vision of Florence, rather the optical, atmospheric vision to be found in Flemish painting. In this work we find Veneziano's most important contribution to later Florentine art, something he certainly imported with him from Venice, a sensuous joy derived by the use of rich brocades and velvets, chromatic jewellery and finery, the joy to the eye which Venice has always and will always exercise on its people and its visitors.

25 – DOMENICO VENEZIANO
Madonna with Child and Saints
Uffizi Museum — Florence

In 1438 Domenico Venziano wrote from Perugia a letter to Piero de' Medici asking him for some work of importance where he would do 'wonderful things'. Proud words of an already established master who had worked in the palace of the powerful Baglioni in Perugia and now longed to vie, in Florence, with the painters for whom he declared his admiration in that very letter: Angelico and Lippi. He was eventually invited to Florence and entrusted with the extremely important cycle of frescoes for the Church of S. Egidio alas destroyed in the 18th century. He worked at this project from 1439 — 1451 with Andrea del Castagno and Alessio Baldovinetti. Among their assistants were Piero della Francesco and Antonio Pollaiolo. In that work, we learn from Vasari, the real Veneziano, great painter of the Renaissance, was formed.

The only work left to suggest what the frescoes must have been like is the Uffizi Altarpiece. Dated between 1445 — 1448, in it the rich pictorial materials of the previous work (ill. 24) are thinned down in the light to their pure essence in order to construct, with the example of Angelico's limpid spatial rhythm, the encircling architectural forms: columns, porticoes, esedras around the solid harmonious figures of the Virgin and Saints.

But the architectural elements are complicated by multiple planes and embellished by marble, pretexts for setting polichrome expanses side by side, a game of colour relations that uses even complementaries to sparkle each other off.

Light however becomes the real vehicle of this work, in its trail it brings life and sparkles relations of intense feeling between mother and child, of sympathy and religious understanding between the others. It is the vehicle which reveals truth and substance, the things and the people that reality is made of.

26 – DOMENICO VENEZIANO
Saint John the Baptist and Saint Francis
Museum of the Opera of Santa Croce — Florence

In this part of a lost fresco, Domenico shows his development towards a more realistic and volumetric rendering of his characters. The influence of Andrea del Castagno is certainly evident in the use of the line, strong, incisive, which seems almost to carve the figures out of the plaster.

The two Saints, each represented in their particular vestement, the goat's skin, symbol of the Baptist's life wandering in the wilderness and Saint Francis' simple cloth gathered by a rope, the poorest vestement he could think of, appear emaciated by their holy vigils and personal privations. And yet their faces are filled with a luminous quality, almost lifting them already beyond the limitations of their physical existence.

Even in this more realistic harsher manner, Veneziano's art stems from the dialogue between light and shade. The light eventually prevailing, as it pervades all his works with a serene optimism.

27 – PIERO DELLA FRANCESCA
Polyptich of the Misericordia, central panel
Town Museum — Sansepolcro

We find Piero for the first time as assistant to Domenico Veneziano on the fresco cycle for the Church of S. Egidio in Florence. Little is known of his earlier apprenticeship, except, it seems that he worked for a short time under Beato Angelico. The two masters mentioned here could be sufficient explanation of Piero's total absorption in his artistic subjects, derived from Angelico, while his modelling of the figures through the use of light could be seen as a derivation from Domenico.

The Madonna shown here, the first work of Piero on his return to his home town in the 1440's, is one of his masterpieces. Domical in form, acting almost as a chapel in the ample embrace of her cloak, open to shelter the believers, she is perhaps the greatest example of an idealised Renaissance realism. So strong is her physical presence, so definite her stand in the centre of the panel, that she seems almost to take it over. The space of the panel is completely taken over by her spread and all that remains around her is the reverberation of her own light.

Piero's use of the gold ground, in absolute reversal of the gold gothic grounds, is space, is atmosphere. Piero subtly opposes it to the black foreground, itself almost a denial of space which tends to throw the believers more closely under the Virgin's protective arms. Among the people at her feet, historians have tended to see the resemblance of people from the artist's home town and some members of his own family. It is interesting to note that Piero was one of the first artists who used models and small wax figures on which he hung draped fabrics to observe from nature the exact falling of clothes on people.

28 – PIERO DELLA FRANCESCA
The Flagellation
National Gallery of the Marche — Urbino

The panel here reproduced is a marvellous example of the interest shown by Piero della Francesca in renaissance perspective, accentuated by the use of a strong foreshortening and by the steep diminution of the chequered floor suggests a vast space.

The reason for this treatment is to effectively isolate the flagellation taking place in the background, from the three characters in the front of the picture.

Their presence in the picture has not been convincingly explained. At times they have been identified with Oddantonio da Montefeltro, the tyrannical Lord of Urbino and his two cruel advisors. The three were eventually murdered by the townsfolk for their atrocious deeds. If this was so, the flagellation taking place in the background could refer to their unjust cruelty to the poor citizens.

Whatever the meaning, the composition is a marvellous example of a classical scene. Almost as in a sacred representation the action takes place as a ritual, no dramatic sequence disturbs the classical solemnity of the poised figures. A moment of actuality can only be detected in the three frontal characters, in the wind that ruffles their clothes, in their up to date costumes, which can certainly be dated to the early 15th century, in clear opposition to the other characters who seem to be wearing Roman tunics.

29 – PIERO DELLA FRANCESCA
Victory of Constantine from the Legend of the True Cross, detail
Church of S. Francesco — Arezzo

In a series of frescoes for the Church of San Francesco Piero illustrated the Legend of the Holy Cross. The work took place between 1455 and 1465 when the artist had reached his full maturity. The frescoes demonstrate it.

In this detail we see Emperor Constantine during the battle that made him the winner over Maxentius. The victory had been pre-announced to him in his sleep when an angel had appeared showing the cross and saying 'in hoc signum vincis' — you will win in the sign of the cross.

The Emperor advances here with the symbolic cross outlined on his hand against the sky, looking at it with absolute faith. Close to this demonstration of an almost medieval belief, the strong realism with which Piero depicts figures and animals brings us suddenly into the full realisation of having entered a new era. The horses are not the metaphysical animals of Paolo Uccello but real living creatures. We can almost follow their panting and pulling at the mouth in their attempts to set off. Their eyes are charged with their sentiment of fidelity and obedience to the master they serve.

Notice also Piero's extremely fine handling of the metal armour, the sharp cuts and creases of the hard metal, its gleams and reflections resplendent in the sun.

30 – PIERO DELLA FRANCESCA
Battle of Cosroe from the Legend of the True Cross, detail
Church of San Francesco — Arezzo

This detail is taken from another section of the frescoes with the Legend of the True Cross. In this scene the artist describes the battle between the Persian King Cosroe and Emperor Eraclius. Cosroe had come into possession of the wood from the True Cross on which Jesus had died, and as a symbol of power, had placed it on his throne. Emperor Eraclius defeated him in a battle by the Danube and at the Persian's refusal to be converted, he followed by severing his head from his body. He then brought back the Cross to Jerusalem, where it was returned to the Holy Sepulchre.

Here almost at the conclusion of the long cycle, Piero is at the end of his labours. In this last figure of a man totally absorbed in the stupour of his own vision, obviously a divine apparition, we can almost sense the feeling of wonder, of incredulity turned into belief, still resisting and yet won.

Piero's powerful sense of volume, his mastery over the rendering of anatomy, foreshortenings and the bold play of light and shade that almost seems to carve the figure out of the wall contributes to our real participation in the story.

91

31 – PIERO DELLA FRANCESCA

Head of a Saint, Saint Julian (?), detail (attributed)
Sansepolcro — Town Museum

The fresco came to light only in 1954, while works were being carried out in the Church of Sant'Agostine in Sansepolcro. The head appeared in the Church's abside as part of a group, perhaps a Sacred Conversation piece which has alas disappeared.

It was immediately attributed to Piero by most of the critics who accepted it as a work from the mature period of the artist about 1460 — just after the completion of the Arezzo cycle.

The head of the Saint is so powerfully painted, with such conviction of expression in the intense stare, the unhesitating modelling of the pronounced lips and chin, as to be a miracle of three dimensional rendering on a flat surface. The work is almost a manifesto of all that the first Renaissance artists had stood for. Piero's use of solid colours, only altered in their intensity by their exposure to light, is typical of his uncluttered, logical compositions.

32 – BENOZZO GOZZOLI
The Adoration of the Kings, detail
Palazzo Medici Riccardi — Florence

In 1461 Cosimo de Medici commissioned Benozzo Gozzoli to paint an Adoration of the Kings all around the walls of his family Chapel in the newly built Medici Palace in Florence. In this painting the whole Medici family had to be represented, with present and past members, four generations of successful representatives of Florentine society, starting with Giovani, Cosimo's father, who had died in 1423. By the time the fresco was completed in 1473, not only Cosimo but his own son Piero had died and the young Lorenzo the Magnificent had taken the threads of Florentine politics under his control.

In this detail, Lorenzo's younger brother Guiliano, aged 16, appears on his own favourite berberry horse, richly attired in a gold trimmed blue tunic. He is holding on the leash a cheetah from the Medici's own zoo. A love for the exotic and oriental fabrics and patterns can be detected in the rich costumes of knights and spectators, even in the extremely decorative horse fineries. Perhaps this was a lingering of the international gothic style which had been practise in Florence side by side with the Renaissance all through the first part of the 15th century, but also the expression of the florentine fashion and taste under the leadership of Lorenzo the Magnificent.

Benozzo Gozzoli an artist who carefully records Florentine lifestyle and way of living of the latter part of the 15th century, in his brightly coloured charming compositions has left us almost a chronicle of the historical period in which he lived.

33 – SANDRO BOTTICELLI

Virgin with Child and Angels, detail
Museum of Capodimonte — Naples

The influence of Filippo Lippi and Andrea Verrocchio in this work of Botticelli are so strong as to date it not later than 1468 when the artist, aged 23, was still working in Verrocchio's workshop. His interest in the rendering of the three dimensional elements of the composition, suggested by a strong play of light and shade however, is somehow contrary to the later development of Botticelli's style.

The Madonna enclosed in a walled garden, gracefully seated, inclines her head as she bends to take the baby from the arms of the little angels who are holding it. The elegant folds of the foreground angel's sleeve and the virgin's tunic, the rich patterns of the gold haloes, the angels wings picked by speckles of gold, all contribute to animate the picture surface, bringing out those values of line and surface on which the artist will concentrate more and more.

This is one of the most beautiful Madonnas of Botticelli's youth, a masterpiece of chromatic values and compositional arrangements.

34 – SANDRO BOTTICELLI
The Adoration of the Kings, detail
Uffizi Gallery — Florence

This detail from one of the most famous of Botticelli's Adoration of the Kings, shows an unusual aspect of the art of Botticelli. The architectural details and his strong power of suggesting vast spaces and great depth, which he will abandon in his later mythological compositions, show him as a complete renaissance artist.

The contrast that he brings out by opposing the ruins of a huge classical temple, to the rustic frame of a shed where the Nativity had taken place, adds interest to the conventional scene of the Adoration. The small figures in the background have an almost impromptu quality which we will find in 17th century Venetian art, in the paintings of Canaletto, Guardi and Piazzetta.

The figures in the foreground however are boldly and plastically rendered. In this illustration we can see the portrait of the man who commissioned the work, Giovanni di Zanobi del Lama, a Florentine money lender, very close to the Medici. He looks straight at us from the centre of our illustration. But the whole picture is filled with portraits of the Medici and their entourage, the scholars and relatives of the powerful family. Botticelli, closely attached to them, appears also in one of the characters.

35 – SANDRO BOTTICELLI
The Annunciation, detail
Belveder Fortress, Florence

This is part of a fresco that Botticelli painted in 1481 in the Hospital of San Martino above the tomb of its founder, Cione Pollini. It was later removed, restored and finally moved to its present location.

The Annunciation, divided into two completely separate sections by a double line of pilasters which separate the garden from the Virgin's room, presents bold foreshortening and daring spatial arrangements. The Angel coming in at a steep angle from the arched door frame, because of the door's slanted viewpoint, seems almost to burst into the garden. A golden light marks his swift progress. The movement is further accentuated by the two circles of inlaid marble on the floor.

The background and the vivid architectural details, all rendered very realistically through the use of a subtle chromatic scheme for which each background colour is re-echoed in the foreground, seem to restate the surface values of the art of painting at times neglected in Renaissance works. The emphasis on representing reality as through a window frame, which Alberti advocated to the Renaissance painters, often made them neglect the overall beauty which a painting should always have as a surface arrangement. Botticelli's Spring is the culmination of Botticelli's attempt to reinstate surface values.

36 – SANDRO BOTTICELLI
Story of St. Ignacius
Uffizi Gallery, Florence

The panel is one of seven parts of the predella of San Barnaba's Altarpiece, painted by Botticelli for the Church of that Saint in Florence. In this composition, the artist illustrates the legend of Saint Ignacius who was tortured and killed by order of Emperor Trajan because he refused to abjure the Catholic Faith. Having told the Emperor that he could not erase from his heart the name of Jesus, after his death, the heart was removed from his body. On it, printed in golden letters was the name of the Redeemer.

Botticelli has chosen a most revolutionary composition, where the sobriety of the structural elements is matched by the restrained use of colour. The story is almost abstracted into its essentials, and yet how eloquent is the message.

The surface of the painting is a miracle of pattern disposition that develops smoothly along the modulation of the variegated strip. The play of the reds and blacks, relieved by touches of gold and white, alternate like the high and low pitches of a pure simple melody.

37 – SANDRO BOTTICELLI
The Birth of Venus, detail
Uffizi Gallery, Florence

In this last illustration of Botticelli's art, a detail from the Birth of Venus, the artist has achieved the perfect expression of his artistic message.

In the complete panel we see Zephyr, the warm wind of spring who carries in the impetus of his warm embrace Chloris, the naked mymph, a personification of the earth in winter. The handsome wind blows Venus towards the shore, where the nymph Ora is expecting her with a flowery cloak spread open in welcome.

The symbolic meanings of the classical story from Ovid, may be many if we follow the interpretations of the humanist scholar friends of the Medici family. Venus could represent Humanitas, the goddess of wisdom, intellectual pursuits and spiritual beauty and the artist with this work might have been recommending to his patron to follow those virtues she represented. This was Lorenzo the Magnificent's cousin, Lorenzo de Pierfrancesco de Medici, a young man orphaned at a very early age. However, if we are to look at this painting as an artistic expression of the Florentine Renaissance, the Birth of Venus remains to us, even through a glimpse of a detail of the whole compositions, the triumph of Venus, goddess of love and beauty, of spring yearnings and man's desires.

In this painting, one of the first works of the Renaissance to represent an enticing feminine nude, Botticelli uses images of great classical beauty. Look at the perfect features of Chloris, enriched by an innocent countenance, at her splendid torso. Observe the delicate single rose silhouetted against the blue ground of the sky, the sea or zephyr's tunic, his free flowing hair streaked by this swift flight through the air and the perfect correspondence of the wind and nymph enlaced in an embrace that only nature, in its combination of the elements, could achieve.

105

38 – ALESSIO BALDAVINETTI
Virgin and Child
Louvre

In this Virgin and Child classically balanced at the centre of the composition, framed by an harmonious landscape of gently curving hills and waterways, Baldovinetti marks the divisive point between early and High Renaissance.

The time of experiments and discoveries, success and failure in art are over. The Renaissance has blossomed into the most serene, self assured artistic expression. Serenely classical, but also responding to its own time of natural and scientific curiosity and discoveries, the art of the mature Renaissance enjoys the full understanding of the nature it expresses.

In this painting we see one of the most beautiful images of the Virgin ever to be painted. Silhouetted in a landscape where the Arno valley appears framed by the Tuscan hills, the Virgin — suave and stately — her hands in prayer, looks adoringly at her baby. The perfect oval of her face, the shape of her neckline, the curve of her shoulders, all harmonize sympathetically with each other and are re-echoed in the undulating hilly background.

The transparent veil which frames her face and the iridescent luminosity of her skin, picked out by the clouds on the horizon, bring the painting to a pitch of technical and chromatic perfection.

39 – DOMENICO GHIRLANDAIO
Double Portrait of Grandfather and Grandchild
Louvre Museum, Paris

In this magnificent Double Portrait by Ghirlandaio we have another example of perfect nature and perfect sentiment. The artist has achieved such unity of composition, such sympathy between content and form, as to make it impossible to distinguish one from the other.

In the panel, the absolutely symmetric frame of the window seems to contain and reinforce the embrace in which the child and the man are linked, in a relation of reciprocal unequivocal tenderness. Here, each element of the composition, the human, the architectural and the natural combine with each other in a flow of sentiment which turns into parts of the same organism.

The sober chromatism, on a scale of reds and darks, reminds us of Botticelli's 'Story of St. Ignacius'. If we eliminate the natural element to be seen behind the window frame, we find that the foreground is composed very much along the same lines. The geometric structure of the architecture lends to the human characters and to the expression of their feeling a timelessness which defies human frailty.

40 – FILIPPINO LIPPI
Scenes from the Life of St Philip the Apostle
Church of S. Maria Novella, Strozzi Chapel — Florence

Filippino, the son of Filippo Lippi and apprentice of Botticelli, was very famous indeed during his lifetime. Lorenzo the Magnificent called him 'the new Apelles', perhaps more a hopeful than a truthful observation. His religious compositions, his Madonna and child themes, follow quite closely — almost to the point of imitation — the works of his master. Nonetheless he never achieves his perfect sense of form and rhythm, his pure aesthetic quality.

In this scene, from a fresco cycle on the Life of Saint Philip the Apostle, Filippino Lippi even using the sumptuous colour of Botticelli with a certain finesse and sensitivity, nervously brings it all to the surface, crowding every element of the story in a frenzied compositive rhythm.

As it has been observed by the Italian critic Luciano Berti, in the fantasy filled episodes of the Strozzi Chapel, Filippino offers us the absurd and wonderful sight of his spasmodic animation of ornaments, architecture, of incredibly lavish clothes, in which the figures seem to contort themselves, never liberated by the clarity of a sure lyrical inspiration.

Here all the figurative culture of the Florentine 15th century becomes nothing but mise-en-scene of a drama already represented.

41 – FILIPPINO LIPPI

The Death of Lucretia, detail
Pitti Palace, Florence

In this detail from the panel of the 'Death of Lucretia' the knight who arrives to witness the tragic event, is beautifully isolated from the rest of the composition by the unadorned geometric planes of the wall. As he enters from a shaded into a marvellously luminous zone, the artist psycologically tries to convey the knight's state of unawareness soon to be changed into one of tragic consciousness.

The chromatic elegance of the scene developed into a series of different tonalities of yellow, only interrupted by the discreet patches of green, black and red of the man's costume, demonstrates what Filippino could be in his best, more intimate artistic expressions.

42 – PIERO DI COSIMO
Simonetta Vespucci
Musee Conde, Chantilly

This portrait represents Simonetta Vespucci, the young daughter of a family of Genovese aristocrats who at the age of 16 came to Florence as a bride to a member of the Vespucci family.

Piero di Cosimo uses this portrait of Simonetta, which he painted posthumous, to symbolise death. In the most poetical and delicate manner, correspondent to the character of the sitter, this artist — often the prophet of doom and apocalyptic tragedies of the human race — rises in sympathetic understanding to a perfect rendering of Simonetta and what she had stood for.

Dead at 21, she had been a radiant impersonification of the Florentine renaissance. The platonic inspirer of Giuliano de Medici, of the poems of Pulci and Politian — Lorenzo's favourite poets — of many of Botticelli's goddesses, her life was cut short by a sudden illness. The whole of Florence had grieved for her in silence.

Piero here, in the bare nature that surrounds her, translates the town's silent grief. The hills re-echo the bare shoulders and the curve of the shawl; but no warmth emanates from the shawl, no flowers charm the slopes' of the hills. The classical profile of Simonetta and her white luminous skin, however, speak of purity and innocence. Her eyes staring outside the picture frame, towards the sky, tell not of despaire aristocrats who at the age of 16 came to Florence as a bride to a member of the Vespucci family.

Piero di Cosimo uses this portrait of Simonetta, which he painted posthumous, to only of hope.

But the black cloud which repeats her profile, the black adder closing around her neck, tell us the sad story of her death.

SIMONETTA IANVENSIS VESPVCCIA

115

43 – LEONARDO DA VINCI
The Adoration of the Kings
Uffizi Gallery, Florence

The painting was commissioned to Leonardo in 1481 by the Monks of San Donato. It remained unfinished by the artist when he left Florence in 1482 to settle in Milan at the court of Lodovico Sforza.

For an Adoration of the Kings, the subject is treated in an entirely new way. None of the familiar characters of the Adoration are to be found here, at least not in their usual position. The shed which is meant to have received Mary and Joseph on that first Night has disappeared, only a slender, verdent tree seems to shelter Mary and her baby. What Leonardo has effectively done is to eliminate all past iconographies and to build a-new the story of the Adoration.

In the centre, almost in isolation, Mother and Baby are set on a plinth or a natural elevation of the ground. The light emanating from them adds to their isolated prominent position but also draws in the main characters of the story. The three Kings looking more like old sages are bent in adoring postures hardly daring to come too close to the divine source of light.

Around them are pressing not the angels and shepherd of the gospel story in their joyful attitudes but a vast crowd of humanity — philosophers, knights divine messengers, beautiful women, young and old. In other words, all humanity is there astounded, questioning, meditating on this arrival that was to disturb the whole known order. The high pitched description of the foreground, is maintained in the background where the procession of the Kings, in its slow progress through the countryside, creates equal commotion.

The architectural background of what must have been a ruined temple, with two interrupted staircases leading nowhere, acts as a magnificent backdrop. It expands the space of the foreground towards vast distances, supporting its elevated theme by the high structures and pilasters reaching almost to the sky. The curved motives, prevalent in the shapes and figures and the ground, are re-echoed by the arches underneath and to the side of the staircases.

44 – MICHELANGELO BONARROTI
The Holy Family
Uffizi Gallery, Florence

The painting, often called the Tondo Doni, was documented in the possession of the Doni family of Florence all through the 16th and 17th century. We do not know when it was commissioned to the artist and historians do not agree on the date of its execution. It must be placed however between 1503 and 1507 when the artist left Florence for Rome to start work on the Sistine Ceiling. By this time Michelangelo had already carved the marble Pietá of St. Peter and two marble tondos — the Taddei Tondo of the Royal Academy in London and the Pitti Tondo of the Uffizi. They both deal with the theme of Mother and Child.

The Doni Tondo is the first painting we have by Michelangelo and his first treatment of the Holy Family. It is often criticised for being more like a piece of sculpture than a painting. In Florence however, at that time, all artists strived in their paintings to render strong plastic effects. Furthermore Michelangelo is creating a masterpiece of pictorial values, both in his chromatic contrasts and in the magnificent compositional link between foreground and background.

The Virgin, having finished her reading, turns to Joseph who gives her the baby to hold. It is a very simple human theme. The symbolic meaning is in the magnificent knot which intertwines the three figures, the baby being the reason for the father and mother coming together. The group of background athletic nudes, besides reiterating the artist's interest in the human figure and his close study of classical prototypes, is there to contrast the pagan era, before Christ's birth, with the present one. The small St. John adoringly looking towards his Saviour, links present and past in its unavoidable conjunction.

45 – MICHELANGELO BUONARROTI
The Holy Family, detail
Uffizi Gallery, Florence

This close up of the previous illustration (n.44) shows the careful attention to detail which Michelangelo lavished on his background scenes. The nude male figures show the great attention that is given to their anatomies. Each muscle is vividly brought out by highlights and we can see how Michelangelo builds up his volumes by the careful use of light and shade. These effects, of course when seen from a distance appear more muted and the overall image is one of unified three dimensionality. At this time in Florence Michelangelo was carrying out his first experiments in vivisection and we can recognise in these figures the application of his own findings.

The treatment of these nudes will be of great importance to the artist in his frescoes of the Sistine Ceiling. Some of the naked youths supporting, with the help of long draperies the large medallions at either sides of the creation panels, are certainly close relations to the ones appearing here.

The little S. John with his beautiful features, bulging cheeks and curly hair remains a resplendent image of innocence and hope.

46 – RAFFAELLO SANZIO
The Tempi Madonna
Alte Pinakothek, Munich

In the Tempi Madonna composed by Raphael around 1508 we find one of the most assured statements of the artist's Mother and Child theme, a theme repeatedly treated by him in continuous iconographic variations. The wish of Raphael for originality was all the time checked by his need for classical, perfectly balanced and harmonious forms, expressive of the subject's feelings through the subtle arrangement of every one of them.

This Madonna elegantly clothed according to early 16th century fashion is nonetheless lacking any embellishment or ornamentation. The ample sweep of her cloak around her hips starts a spiralling movement which continues throughout the picture up to the two heads of Mother and child held together almost as if by an invisible thread. Suavely modelled, the flesh of the baby and the resplendent complexion of the mother add a physical, sensual touch, to the free expression of their sentiment.

47 – RAFFAELLO SANZIO
Portrait of Agnolo Doni
Pitti Palace — Florence

The portrait of Agnolo Doni is one of a series of portraits which the artist executed during his Florentine sojourn between 1501 and 1508.

The sitter, a member of a well known Florentine family of humanists and art collectors — and the owners of Michelangelo's Tondo of the Holy Family (ill. 44) — was both patron and friend of Raphael.

He is represented here in classical frontal pose, resting on the marble parapet of a balcony perhaps in his Florentine palace. He sits silhouetted against a sympathetic but artificial sky. The detail of the books under his arm suggests he is a man of culture while the elegant hand with the cameo ring shows him as a man of taste. Spreading across the canvas with consummate ease, Agnolo is the embodiment of Florentine sophistication at the beginning of the 16th century.

In this portrait, almost for the first time, Raphael attempts a fine psychological rendering of the subject's mind. His sensitive features, the inquiring but almost dreamy look point to the many hours spent in intellectual speculation.

48 – RAFFAELLO SANZIO
Portrait of Maddalena Doni
Pitti Palace, Florence

The sitter is Maddalena Strozzi who married Agnolo Doni (ill. 47) in 1503. Both portraits were believed to have been painted for their wedding, but recently the critics have dated them around 1507, with the portrait of Agnolo perhaps a little earlier than the more three dimensional one of Maddalena.

Raphael shows here his indebtedness to Leonardo. The sitter's pose brings immediately to mind the Mona Lisa which Leonardo was painting in Florence around 1503. However something in the subject's appearance or character must have slightly impaired the artist's inspiration. According to the Renaissance insistence on the truthful rendering of nature, however, the portrait is a miracle of character-rendering.

This being said, the composition is magnificent. Maddalena sits opulent and voluminous in front of a window opening on a florentine summer evening. The colours of her complexion and of her azure tunic are picked out and continued in the background landscape. The beautiful curve of her full shoulders is itself extended and continued by the darker line of the distant hills. Raphael's rendering of fabrics and different textures is sharpened into what will become one of the most exquisite technical qualities in his pictures.

49 – RAFFAELLO SANZIO
Portrait of a Lady
National Gallery of the Marche, Urbino

One of the last portraits of Raphael's Florentine period, the sitter has not been identified to this date. The portrait continues that firm exploration of the human character which we saw first in the portrait of Agnolo Doni.

The young woman, by the sensitive if somewhat enigmatic expression, shows a spiritual intelligence as one of her distinguishing features. Extremely noble in the classical pose which emphasises regularity and symmetry in both the sitter and her arrangement in space, the artist's subtle use of the decorative elements, which are reduced to their absolute essentials towards the top of the picture, allows the bare shoulders and spiritual head to stand out alone as the painting's focal point. The central axis of the picture, along which all elements seem to converge, is strongly emphasised. Starting in the middle of her face along her classical nose, it is continued in the hanging pendant with the cross and finally in the sitter's hand. The strong vertical leads our eyes back and forth along this visual path, making us at all times conscious of the full presence of the sitter.

50 – RAFFAELLO SANZIO
Portrait of a Woman
Pitti Palace, Florence

This portrait, one of the last of Raphael's Florentine period, was discovered only at the beginning of the 18th century. It is called 'La Gravida' — the pregnant woman, perhaps because of the woman's protruding stomach to which she unequivocally points. It may have been a portrait to celebrate the sitter's future motherhood.

Raphael's 'Gravida' may be considered the masterpiece in his newly achieved maturity. Its self-assured reality affirming itself it is enclosed, nonetheless, in a formal perfection no reality can reach. It can clearly be seen in the simple masses of the head, the bust, the large damask sleeve, in which one can detect a modelling tension made so insistent, so subtle as to rival, if not to surpass, the rarefied play of shadow in Leonardo's shading.

This painting is a marvellous example of tonal rather than local colour. The picture is all on the tonality of flesh pinks. Starting from her face, any other surface is only a tonal variaton of the same colour. The few white elements which appear in the painting are all streaked with pink so as not to stand out against such soft chromatic orchestration. The volumetric full rendering of the sitter's forms, amply set against the black background that rather then deny, creates space, anticipates Raphael's grandiose compositions of the Roman period.

51 — JACOPO CARRUCCI, called PONTORMO

Ventunno and Other Divinities, from the fresco of Ventunno and Pomona, detail
Medici Villa, Poggio a Caiano

Jacopo Pontormo, the first and most original of the Florentine Mannerists, was apprenticed in the workshops of Leonardo, Piero di Cosimo and Andrea del Sarto. The greatest influence on his art however came from the heroic, bold compositions of Michelangelo's maturity.

In this work, part of a wall decoration which the artist executed around 1519-21 for the Medici in their country villa at Poggio a Caiano, Michelangelo's background in the Tondo Doni (Ill. 45) has certainly been the source of inspiration.

The frescoes, commissioned by Pope Leo X in commemoration of his father Lorenzo the Magnificent, with their arcadian theme of country relaxation and the ease of mind associated with it was certainly an ideal theme to represent the Magnifico. In the latter part of his life, Lorenzo who wrote many arcadic poems in celebration of country life, spent more and more of his time in his Villa at Poggio a Caiano.

In this part of the fresco, just by the Michelangesque nude stretching in a pose that loses the classical character of its predecessor, appears what is meant to be a self portrait of the artist who has aged himself to fit the part of the old peasant.

52 – JACOPO CARRUCCI, called PONTORMO
Pomona and Other Divinities, from the fresco of Ventunno and Pomona, detail
Medici Villa, Poggio a Caiano

This is the other half of the fresco from the previous illustration, (ill. 51) or its feminine counterpart. In traditional country fashion, Pontormo separates the female members of the group from the male. Artistically the contrast is most pleasing. The artist continues to contrast with chromatic consistency, so that on a bed of browns and greens, we find blue as the main tonality on the left, while oranges and bronzes grace the right section.

Relaxing in overemphasised classical poses, with great use of contrapposto not only within the same figure, but by opposing front and back of two contiguous figures, the artist creates a magnificent compositive rhythm. Obviously happy amidst a profusion of fruits and foliage, the agrarian divinities spend their time in easy relaxation. They are practising the 'Otium' or holiday, advocated by Cicero for a healthy mind.

The theme and the treatment stems from classicity, and yet, the unconventionality of the poses and of the setting, reveal that reaction to the classical formulas of Leonardo, Raphael and Michelangelo's art, which will become the most relevant aspect of Pontormo's art.

53 – JACOPO CARRUCCI, called PONTORMO
The Deposition, detail
Church of S. Felicita, Florence

This detail from the Deposition, one of Pontormo's more mature works, was painted by the artist as part of the decoration of a Chapel in the Church of Santa Felicita which was bought by Ludovico Capponi in 1525.

Having been entrusted with the complete decoration of the site, Vasari informs us that Pontormo worked for three whole years in absolute secrecy. Not even his client was allowed to see the works during their progress.

In truth, some of Pontormo's best compositions are to be found in this chapel. The Deposition is the real masterpiece, however. To give more solemnity and increase the pathos of this Deposition the artist amplifies the forms and weaves together lines and masses in an incredible rhythm, suspended like a cloud in an unreal space.

The colour is now intensified without shadows, in over-acute relations of pinks, tenuous purples and translucent blues.

54 – JACOPO CARUCCI, called PONTORMO
The Visitation
Carmignano, Pieve di San Michele

In this panel painted around 1530 the artist continues the style developed in his decoration for the Church of S. Felicita (ill. 53).

The amplification of the forms is further extended. The four figures pushed in the very foreground seem to take it over, while the architecture — two wings of a scenario — are placed at such a steep angle as to effectively squeeze the characters out of the picture's space. The wings act only as a foil against which each figure is chromatically contrasted. To a lighter fabric is opposed a darker wall, to the brightest pink of the woman to the left of the Virgin is contrasted the deepest mauvy green.

Mary and St. Anne finally united to share the joy of the great news, are shown only as magnificent forms, each curve, each fold, each angle picked out and contrasted by an opposing one in the other figure. This play of shapes is intensified by the play of colour and light equally opposed and contrasted — simpler in the older woman, full of incidents and drama in the Virgin.

The intense expressions in the face of these two women is emphasised by the cold unmovable features of the ones behind them. They appear as two tragic masques from a greek theatre, silent but looming witnesses to what happens in front of them. In these cool shades of colour, in these iced expressions and frozen grimaces, the lyrical sentiment of the Renaissance masters is certainly forgotten, and yet out of their formal achievements another summit is reached in the enigmatic aestheticism of this great mannerist.

55 – ROSSO FIORENTINO
Moses and the Daughters of Jetro, detail
Uffizi Gallery, Florence

In 1512, when Pontormo entered the last studio of his apprenticeship the one of Andrea del Sarto, he must have met Rosso Fiorentino.

This last painter had entered del Sarto's studio after having left many masters 'since his own opinion was contrary to their manner'. Rosso's formation, as Pontormo's, was indebted to Michelangelo, but something in Raphael's interest for colour must have found a special response in our artist. Colour will become his paramount interest, the thread with which he will weave his artistic cloth.

In the composition of the biblical story of Moses, saving the daughters of Jetro, a disturbing violence is unleashed in the rendering of the man's fight. A Michelangeolesque, titanic expression of force unravels on the panel where the bodies are spread, hurt or ready to hurt. The composition is held together by a magnificent pyramidal arrangement, where the body of one man is the apex, while the base is made of a long tangle of bodies. This Michelangelo-like form, however, is almost devoid of its weight and substance the moment light and colour intervene. The form decomposes into fantastic chromatic solids, while the running women in the background appear as vivid streaks of colour enlight like unreal fireworks.

141

56 – ANGELO DI COSIMO, called BRONZINO
The Archangel Saint Michael, detail of vault
Chapel of Eleanor of Toledo, Palazzo Vecchio, Florence

The detail is from the ceiling in the Chapel of Eleonora, Duchess of Florence. The vault is decorated with representations of the Four Saints.

In our illustration, Saint Michael in theatrical pose is fighting with the devil. Bronzino's admiration for Michelangelo's treatment of human anatomy and his heroic, romantic manner of rendering it, is obvious in the complacent execution of the Saint's torso.

A sense of ambiguity, often present in the painting of Bronzino is recognisable here, where the torso although rendered naturalistically, is nonetheless closer to a dummy than a real being. Halfway between the male and female form, it is identified with the St. Michael only because of his head and limbs which are treated with absolute propriety.

The blue of the background, lifeless and icy, brings out by contrast the rounded baby forms of the putto and the opposed natures of the most beautiful angel in the celestial hierarchy and the monstrous devil.

Classical art which arrived at a magical perfection in the rendering of the human form is here turned into a manner, a complacent play where the rules of classic art and proportions, observed up to a point, by some strange twist of the artist's mind are suddenly manipulated to give a feeling of tension, almost of strained sensuality.

57 – ANGELO DI COSIMO called BRONZINO
Portrait of Giannettino Doria (attributed)
Doria Palace, Rome

This portrait of Giannettino Doria, nephew of the famous Italian Admiral Andrea Doria, belongs to Bronzino's Roman period in the 1540's. The work cannot be dated later than 1547, because of the young man's death in a political plot during that year.

The artist, who had already done a portrait of the Admiral, knew that he was interpreting here a youth belonging to one of the most powerful and aristocratic families of Italy, full of ideals, ideas and ready to use his sword.

The air of easy 'nonchalance', the elegant pose, the refined hands and sensitive features, all contribute to build up an interesting human character. Reserved and withdrawn in his privileged world his image, however, does not provoke in us a human response, just admiration.

The unnatural greens and deep reds of the colour scheme are lowered in tonality by the deep black of the young man's cloak, while the picture rail against the plain wall, picked out in green, creates a strong horizontal just above the cloak. This stresses the high focal point of the composition behind the young man's eyes. His stare is thus stretched all over the canvas and becomes the unavoidable point of convergence of the spectator's eyes.

58 – BACHIACCA
The Magdalene
Pitti Palace — Florence

Bachiacca worked in Florence all through the middle of the 16th century, a convinced follower of Pontormo.

In this magnificent chromatic composition the Magdalene is no more the biblical repentant of drastically changed feelings and emotions, but a most ambiguous creature, highly sensitive, perplexed and disturbed. The contrast of colours bring out her complex character.

The bright fiery red, toned down by the beautiful bottle green of the background, lingers in the brighter highlights of the Magdalene's hair. Her eyes, still magnificently alluring, take another significance the moment we notice the holy halo around the crown of her hair.

Attention to details and to atmospheric mood-creating effects is here alternated like the light and shade on the woman's features. The painting moves the beholder to a continuous search for the right meaning. It puzzles the intellect; it satisfies the aesthetic sense.

59 – MIRABELLO CAVALORI
The Wool Factory, detail
Decoration of Francis I Study, Palazzo Vecchio — Florence

One of the last episodes of Mannerist art in Florence is the decoration of the little Study of Francis I, the bizarre son of Cosimo I.

The decoration of the whole palace from the Hall of the Cinquecento to the Ducal apartments had started two decades earlier under the direction of Giorgio Vasari, the first art historian since classical times. With a team of young assistants working under him, the artist, a far greater architect than painter, orchestrated a magnificent series of mythological story tales or classical vignettes all treated in a way that was reminiscent of the art of a Renaissance that was now no more.

Cavalori's 'Wool Factory' deals with a theme of great importance to the economy of Florence in its 15th century boom when the Florentines were the greatest suppliers of wool to the whole of Europe. The subject is now treated as a story from the past. The youths clothed in classical togas, breeches or bathing trunks, could equally be in Roman baths. The activity and the spaces, unclear and cluttered, eliminate however any sense of classical repose and equilibrium in the scene. The artist seems imprisoned in a dream of past forms which have by now lost all meaning.

MIRABELLO · CAVALORI

149

60 – MIRABELLO CAVALORI
The Sacrifice of Lavinia
Decoration of Francis I Study, Palazzo Vecchio — Florence

Another scene from the little Study's decoration. This time a more classical theme with the story of Lavinia, daughter of Agamemnon, who has to be sacrificed to the Gods so that a favourable wind will blow the Greek ships towards the land of Troy.

The composition is organised along an ascending staircase, which is almost always shown at an angle, offering its uneasy spaces to the actors. A very dangerous and uncomfortable stage to perform on! If Raphael's frescoes in the Vatican were the source of inspiration, it also recalls the wide frontal staircase of the School of Athens although it is interesting to note the similarities as well as the differences.

Nonetheless Cavalori with his spatial tension and uncomfortable staging conveys only too well the mixed feelings of Lavinia's father and compatriots, the anguish and uncertainty of the Pagan Faith.

Here the artist achieves an absolute mastery over colour. Look how he pours the vibrant hues of his Homeric tale over the whole scenographic fabric of the classic columns.

151

61 – GIROLAMO MACCHIETTI

The Baths of Pozzuoli
Decoration of Francis I Study, Palazzo Vecchio — Florence

The last page of the Mannerists' uneasy classicism is here written for us by Girolamo Macchietti. Another pupil of Vasari, the master in charge of stage effects and ceremonial apparatus for the Medici.

The spatial effects in this composition are multiplied in almost geometric progression. The continuous shift of visual angle, the groups arranged now horizontally now vertically to the picture plane are only possible in a scene of general character like this. Along these lines the architecture successfully recreates the atmosphere of a Roman bath, its wide spaces, its re-echoing halls, so suggestive and full of illusionary effects to become nowadays the ideal setting for vast choral operas. Cavalori's imagination has certainly had a presentiment of such a modern use. His characters however once again are in slight opposition to the setting. No noble Romans, no orators or senators stretch their limbs on the marble floors, but a population of athletes ready to use their limbs rather than their minds.

Once again the theme is classical but the tension and experiments evident in its rendering are the sure manifestation that classicity is a feeling of the past — the Renaissance is over.